Table of Contents

Appendix 5
Abbreviations Spelled Out
My Story

Introduction

An adult family home is a type of long-term care setting broadly known as "adult foster care." Adult Family Homes have been an active and integral part of the long-term care ecosystem for more than thirty years!

They were developed to provide our elderly with a less-restrictive alternative to institutional nursing home care. Operating in local communities, they offer a choice that allows residents to maintain –and usually *enhance* their quality of life – while receiving personal care services, housekeeping, medications, health-related assistance, and these days, even medical oversight. Often times, residents are able to continue living and receiving needed care without having to move to a different facility or an institution, later in life, making it a fantastic "aging-in-place" option.

While the community has long embraced adult family homes in Washington and in other states, the industry generally receives a low level of public exposure and awareness. I believe this is partially due to the fact that individuals and small business owners – caregivers at heart – mostly run the industry as individual providers. This is in contrast to the deep-pocketed corporations run by well-educated and seasoned business executives. The latter group is obviously more interested in larger assisted living settings.

Nonetheless, adult family care homes are a growing trend and continue to gain popularity amongst seniors who need personal care, not just housing. Most people would rather stay home for as long as possible, but when circumstances no longer permit it, the next best option is often the smaller residential care setting found in an adult family home.

Children of elderly parents value the warmth and intimacy of a real home, and the high degree of personal attention their loved ones receive. Since adult family care homes operate in residential neighborhoods, it's very convenient for loved ones to stop by on a dime, encouraging the maintenance of close relationships and care monitoring. Residents also value the ability to maintain as much independence as possible while benefiting from the immediate availability of personal assistance and care. We call this "as needed care" as opposed to "scheduled care," which is the type of care common to assisted living and larger, more institutional Nursing Homes.

Medical professionals also like adult family homes. In fact, many people first hear of adult family homes through their geriatrician or family doctor, or from social workers and discharge planners during a hospital or nursing home stay. A common phrase I hear from prospective clients is, "The doctor said dad can't go back to the assisted living, and he needs to go to an adult family home."

Local governments also rely on adult family care homes, especially to provide long-term care to seniors who receive state funding (Medicaid). In Washington, it's estimated that the Department of Social and Health Services (DSHS) saves some $240 million per year by using adult family homes rather than more expensive Nursing Homes options.

Adult family care homes have grown significantly over the last 15 years, and the trend continues to point in the same direction. For example, at the time of this writing more than 5 million people are living with Alzheimer's disease (AD) or another type of dementia, and this number could triple by 2050. They need to receive care by skilled and trained caregivers, and adult family homes are a perfect option for many of them.

The purpose of this book is to provide you with a comprehensive overview of Adult Family Homes (AFH), as well as other long-term care options for elderly persons who can no longer live safely on their own. It is written to help you, the caretaker, make an educated and well-informed decision about the best placement for your loved one, even if that placement is not in an adult family home.

Also included are a number of resources such as links to websites, forms, and questionnaires. This information will make it much easier to find the best match for your family's needs.

Other sections include information on:
- How to Tour Facilities
- Facility Types And Their Critical Differences
- Qualifications of Caregivers & Providers in Adult Family Care Homes
- Hospice Care
- What Help is Available When Searching for Care

- Tax Deductions
- How to Monitor for Quality Care and Prevent Abuse

After going through the information and directions in this book, you will have the confidence to take a clear and active role in the care of your loved one and be equipped to handle any concerns with confidence.

Lastly, while I often refer to the State of Washington, you will find that the principles and approaches described here will serve you well regardless of where you live. Personal bias

There is no hiding the fact that I am obviously biased to adult family homes as a great option for long-term care. To start, owning and operating adult family homes is still my primary "bread and butter."

But more importantly, my career as a nurse and care provider has been extremely rewarding over the years, having given me the opportunity to make a marked difference in the lives of hundreds of families and their elderly loved ones. It's given me a strong sense of contribution to my community and the satisfaction of helping so many seniors live richer, more meaningful lives, despite their disabilities and physical frailties.

To strengthen this bias are the countless calls I receive from people at home or in other housing and care settings who suffered significant injuries because they were not receiving the needed care and supervision. My unique perspective lets me see the long-term care industry from the inside out.

But I am also a realist; not all care homes are as good as I wish they were – or a good fit for *you*. I visit Nursing Homes that I find to be excellent, and talk to many people who are very happy in assisted living facilities. Other times though, I see the proverbial *writing on the wall*, in living situations with potentially disastrous consequences.

Despite this bias, my intention is to share what I know as objectively as possible, and if it seems as though I am talking down on other settings, please forgive me, as it's not my intent—I want you to fully understand your options and identify the potential outcomes of your decisions.

How To Use This Book

The entire book can obviously be read start-to-finish if you wish, but this is by no means necessary.

To save you some time, I recommend that you first read the Table of Contents so you can skip right to sections most important to you.

I purposely wrote most of this as standalone, short article-style pieces, and some of the information is repeated in various sections whenever it's relevant so you won't miss a potentially important piece of information if you skip chapters.

About the Author

Joseph Spada, LPN, CGCP

Founder, Spada Homes, Inc.
Founder, Adult Family Homes Central

Joseph Spada is a geriatric nurse and certified geriatric care provider. Blending high quality care standards learned from living and working at the University Hospital in Geneva, Switzerland, family values from his Italian origin and upbringing, and nursing skills acquired in the US, Joseph left the hospital and nursing home world to start adult family care homes in Seattle.

For the last twenty-three years, he has built a reputation for providing outstanding care to the seniors who live in his adult family care homes. He brings families peace of mind through the knowledge that their loved one is being cared for like family, not just a customer or patient.

Joseph served as a board member and past president of the Snohomish-King County Association of Adult Family Home Providers. In the early-to-mid 1990s, he helped form the statewide association of Adult Family Homes in Washington State, the WSRCC (Washington State Residential Care Council).

Joseph is a faculty instructor at Seattle Community College teaching adult family home providers the State-required Administrator Course, covering topics such as licensing and compliance, business operation, staff management, resident care and rights, resident assessments, care planning, and more. He has taught First-Aid and CPR as a Red Cross instructor and tutored nursing students for North Seattle Community College.

Over the years he's counseled and guided hundreds of families in finding and monitoring the personal care of their loved seniors, not just in adult family homes, but in assisted living and Nursing Homes as well.

Joseph maintains a consulting practice for care home providers focused on helping them overcome operational challenges, succeed in the current marketplace, and most importantly, on how to achieve distinction and excellence in their adult family homes.

Why I Wrote This Book

Last years ago, I read an extensive article on long-term care housing options for seniors by an "expert" in the housing industry in Washington State. To my amazement, not a single mention of Adult Family Homes was included. I told myself I had probably missed something, so I re-read the fairly lengthy article and sure enough, not a word about Adult Family Homes.

How, I asked, can an "elder care and housing expert" omit one of the most important long-term care options in Washington State? Since Adult Family Homes are an integral part of Washington's elder care system, caring for nearly 16,000 individuals, I decided it was time to share what I've learned over the last two-plus decades.

This includes writing this book and launching http://www.AdultFamilyHomesCentral.com to help raise public awareness, educate, and provide a method for helping locate the best Adult Family Homes.

Searching online, I continue to be amazed by how little information—or bad information—there is for people looking for Adult Family Homes. No one has taken the time to clearly and simply outline what your options are and the differences between them. No one has taken the time to *educate you* so you can be empowered to make smarter, clearer, and more informed decisions.

Through my involvement with the Washington State Residential Care Council (WSRCC) and the political process in Olympia, Washington, I've witnessed first-hand how politics is the slowest and hardest way to realize positive change. And, more importantly, I've witnessed time and time again how more legislation and regulations resulted in shifting care providers' focus to paperwork to satisfy the state rather than to provide better resident care and services.

Although clearly necessary, more laws and regulations seem to give consumers a false sense of safety, leading them to relinquish a greater amount of personal accountability and responsibility. The real problem is that *some people do bad things regardless of legislation.*

My message to you is simple:

Don't wait or count on someone else to keep your loved one safe. Stay involved and accountable, and remember that you don't have to do it alone. I will show you how to accomplish this as effectively as possible, and in the process maintain or rebuild a healthy relationship as the adult child, not the direct primary caregiver.

Whether you're faced with an immediate crisis or are carefully planning for your future or that of a loved one, it is essential that you choose *for* yourself, but not necessarily *by* yourself.

I hope this book will provide you with guidance and insight into the world of long-term care so you can make clearer and more educated choices about the long-term care facility that best meets your family's needs.

The Family Values Dilemma

Should *you* care for your aging parent or spouse?

There is no "right" answer to this question because everyone's values are unique and different, but I want to offer some food for thought.

Take my mother-in-law Marty. When Marty's mom was no longer able to safely care for herself, Marty enthusiastically raised her hand; "I adore mom, and she did so much for us, I will take care of her myself."

But it wasn't long before Marty's labor of love turned into a full time job, then into an outright nightmare. Mom would call at all hours of the day and night begging for medication. She became more confused and started arguing and dishing out verbal abuse on a regular basis, refusing to eat, to take baths, or even to get dressed.

Marty explains, "I'd make a doctor's appointment, and when I'd show up to pick up mom she'd refuse to go. I was constantly left having to pick up pieces for all the missed appointments, and countless hours of wasted time and effort. Mom would try hiding the fear she felt living alone, and I was afraid because I knew she wasn't getting the care she deserved. She wasn't safe and I became deeply depressed."

Eventually Marty's mom became so ill, weak, and malnourished that she was admitted to the hospital. Once stable she was moved to a nursing home to convalesce and after six months was settled into an Adult Family Home. Initially her mom complained and begged to move back home, but this time Marty knew better and refused to acquiesce. It was a difficult transition for them both, especially with her mom's anger. Marty also felt a good deal of guilt having promised to take care of her mom.

Fast-forward two and-a-half years. As Marty's mom settled into her new room at the Adult Family Home, both of their lives dramatically improved. Her mom is content, well adjusted, very well cared for, and her health well monitored. She feels safe and has new friends. She loves her room and is allowed to spend her days pretty much the way she wants; reading and surrounded by her beloved books.

She still voices an occasional complaint but comments, "What home doesn't have a squabble or two?" As for Marty, she is still very much involved in her mom's life but this time, in ways that leave her with freedom and peace of mind—she feels like her mom's daughter again.

I love Marty's story because it also illustrates the inner struggle that so many adult children feel when caring for a parent. Children struggle with feelings of guilt when they consider placing their parents in a care home or facility— and I get it.

I come from a culture where we care for our own parents, and until recently there were very few other options available. My grandparents on both sides were cared for at home until they passed, and I witnessed my maternal grandfather's last day on this earth at the tender age of two. Many of my aunts and uncles are still caring for in-laws, and my forty-seven year old brother is at home with our parents who are now in their mid-eighties.

But even in my native Italy this is changing rapidly and more elderly than ever are going to care homes and boarding homes – but they avoid Nursing Homes like the plague!

So I know first-hand what it's like to embrace that role as an adult child, and the challenges that come with it. I know what it's like to care for other people's parents as a professional, and what it's like *not* to be in the role of the primary care taker for my own parents.

You may feel that placing your parent or spouse in care facility means you've somehow failed them. Because they cared for you, you have an unspoken obligation to care for them, right?

In many ways, it's an unrealistic expectation we place on ourselves, especially in the American culture. I find that most elderly who have enough cognition to share their thoughts invariably tell me that one of their worst dreads is being a burden to their children.

1. In some cultures such as my native Italy, societal and family structure still supports caring for the elderly at home; children and grandchildren seldom move away to other cities or states, and everyone has (or until recently has had) a clear role… husbands work and wives stay home and provide care to parent

and grandparents. Sisters and cousins offer relief care, while teens and young adults run errands. The culture in America does not operate this way.

2. Most people don't realize caring for a loved one is a full time job and an enormous commitment. They often underestimate the impact it will have on their own lives.

3. In America, most people work full time, which makes them unavailable to provide the necessary care.

4. Most people are not equipped with the nursing and medical knowledge necessary to provide safe and quality care.

5. Parent-child or spousal dynamics often make it more emotionally stressful to provide the care yourself.

The truth is most seniors DO BETTER in small care settings than they do at home. I see it every day in my practice and in the lives of those I help. The elder ends up receiving more competent care, enjoys more social interactions with peers, and gets more attention. Ultimately, this results in a higher quality of life for them—and for you.

I will bet that the quality of your own life and relationship with your parent will be significantly improved when you spend time enjoying each other's company in a parent-child connection, rather than being their primary caregiver. For your parent, having someone to look forward to seeing is very important and gives them a reason to live. Finally, no one will ever care as much as you do for your parent's safety and well-being, and this allows you to serve as their best advocate.

Long-Term Care by the Numbers

Wow, have things changed in the last few years! The good news is that there are ample choices for long-term care – and that's also the bad news.

I find that most people who seek my help with elder care do not understand the essential differences between various types of care settings, what care and services they might expect to receive in each of those settings, or the drawbacks that exist within each type.

The old adage "if all you have is a hammer, everything looks like a nail" applies when exploring housing and care services: each operator wants to sell you on what they offer as the best option! There are also plenty of people with related businesses taking advantage of your unfamiliarity, offering their services and keeping you in relative darkness about how the system really works.

Don't worry though – by the time you've finished this book, you'll know how to assess your loved one's care needs, know which facility type is the best consideration for you based on your needs, what to look for in a facility, how to find the right place, and how to ensure your loved one is getting quality care. You'll also know how to address and resolve any concerns or issues quickly and confidently.

Sound good? Let's get started!

Since the early 1990s, more than 220 retirement housing communities were founded for people 55-and-older in Washington State. Oddly enough, retirement communities and independent senior living facilities *are not state licensed*. These are commonly referred to as "senior housing services."

As far as non-state-licensed facilities are concerned, Continuing Care Retirement Communities (CCRCs) belong in that category. A CCRC is a residential community that offers a range of housing options (from independent living through nursing home care) and varying levels of medical and personal care services. A CCRC is designed to meet changing needs as one grows older. People usually move into them when they're still healthy.

Expect to sign a long-term contract that provides for housing, personal care, housekeeping, yard care and nursing care. This typically involves either a buy-in or entry fee in addition to monthly charges, which may change according to medical or personal care services required. Fees vary depending on whether you own or rent the living space, its size and location, the type of service plan chosen, and the current risk for needing intensive long-term care. Because the contracts are usually life-long and fees vary widely, it is imperative to get financial and legal advice before signing.

As of this writing, there are more than 530 Assisted Living Facilities (in Washington) holding boarding home licenses, some with a Dementia Care specialty. Assisted Living Facilities developed greatly in the last 12 years or so, and just a few large corporations own or operate many, if not most of them. (Emeritus and Sunrise are two well-known examples.)

In the last decade, driven by popular demand, Adult Family Homes have grown from a few hundred to about 2,900 in 2013.

Private in-your-home care providers have grown to some 100 companies, up from only a handful in the early '90s. Many have multiple offices and some are franchises.

The tables below show the number of licensed facilities in Washington State by type and the number of licensed beds for each type of care facility.

Total Number of *Licensed Facilities* in Washington State as of 2012 (approximate)

Adult Family Homes (AFH)	Boarding Homes (BH)	Nursing Homes (NH)	TOTAL
2,883 AFHs	539 BHs	245 NHs	3,667

Adult Family Homes (AFH)Boarding Homes (BH)Nursing Homes (NH)TOTAL

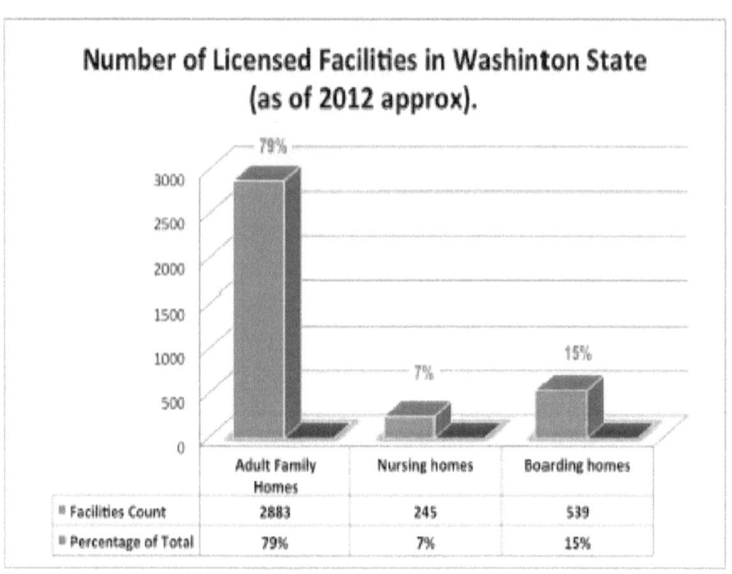

Total Number of Licensed *Beds* in WA as of 2012 (approximate)

Adult Family Homes	Boarding Homes	Nursing Homes	TOTAL
16,057 beds	29,941 beds	22,818 beds	67,831

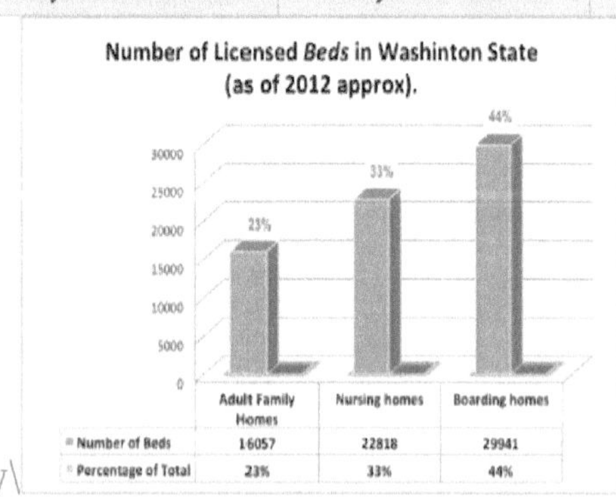

Adult Family\

What are Adult Family Homes (AFHs)?

Adult Family Homes don't simply offer a "home-like" environment – they ARE a home! Although located in residential neighborhoods, they are considered "healthcare facilities" for business, regulatory, and taxation purposes.

In Washington State, they are licensed to serve no more than 6 people per location. The staff-to-resident ratio is usually 1 staff to 6 residents at minimum (and often higher in quality homes). This compares very favorably to Nursing Homes or Assisted Living Facilities, where one caregiver can routinely be assigned 8 to 16 residents, and sometimes even more. During night shifts in assisted living facilities, 1 staff to 30 or more residents is common.

Those who live in Adult Family Homes are not considered patients, but residents. Residents are provided the warmth and familiarity of a home and other residents and caregivers become extended family.

Providing round-the-clock care to approximately 16,000 people in Washington State alone, Adult Family Homes are considered to be the least restrictive and most affordable option in long-term care. Since they save Washington State more than $240 million per year on long-term care costs (via the Medicaid program), the state is highly invested in regulating and maintaining this thriving industry.
While not all Adult Family Homes are created equal, chances are you can find one to suit your needs perfectly. Settings vary from luxurious million-dollar homes with waterfront views to smaller, more modest homes.

You may find private or shared rooms, with or without bathrooms, larger spaces with more privacy, or even assisted-living-like dwellings for residents who are ambulatory and more physically able. With that being said, don't assume that a higher cost or a "fancy" Adult Family Home reflects greater skills, abilities, or quality of care. As with anything, always do your research.

Some AFHs are owned by registered or licensed nurses (RNs or LPNs) or certified nursing assistants (NA-Cs or CNAs), and others may be opened by individuals who first cared for a parent or loved one and then went on to provide care for other seniors. Adult Family Home owners are like extended family members. Sometimes you'll even see their children, pets, and residents all under one roof ... a win for all!

What Services Can I Receive in Adult Family Homes?

Services provided somewhat differ from home-to-home but are generally tailored to meet your loved one's needs. Each provider chooses what services to offer, although in Washington State many services are compulsory, the basic premise being to avoid future relocation.

1. Assistance with personal care including dressing, bathing, incontinence, mobility, and any other personal care;
2. Medication assistance;
3. Vital signs and health monitoring;
4. Memory care for people with dementia and Alzheimer's disease;
5. Hospice services and end-of-life care;
6. Night Care—on call or round-the-clock awake staff;
7. Meals and snacks, including pureed foods, low sodium diets, etc.;
8. Housekeeping and laundry;
9. Nursing, medical and even dental care;
10. Various activities, either provided by the home staff or contracted by third party;
11. Beautician services;
12. Transportation to medical appointments and recreational outings.

Again, the above list represents services that are customarily offered in Adult Family Homes – do your own due diligence, especially with items such transportation.

What Level of Care Can I Get In An Adult Family Home?

As long as state requirements are met (WAC 388-76), care providers can offer as much or as little care as they are capable, qualified, or willing to provide.

If that sounds a bit scary, the law also requires that providers make "reasonable accommodations" to avoid displacing residents when more care is needed, ultimately greatly improving the odds that a resident will be able to stay in the home and age in place.

Many care homes will care for your parent or spouse to the end of life, if that's what you want. Many homes fully manage residents who have severe dementia, are wheelchair bound, bed bound, on Hospice care, are diabetics, have had strokes, or have other debilitating health issues.

Homes that are owned and operated by nurses are typically able to provide care to higher acuity residents (that's a resident who requires more care and has more significant health issues or complications). However, there are plenty of "average-looking" care homes owned by excellent non-nurse caregivers who can provide high levels of care as well. Some investigation and well thought-out questions are critical to determine a facility's level of care capability.

While residing in a home owned by an RN or LPN has obvious benefits, you should be aware that a nurse-owner who also maintains outside employment will have limited time for residents, or they may prefer not to provide nursing care themselves due to liability exposure as a medical professional.
In either case, such a scenario could reduce the benefit to your parent or loved one.

Ask how much care a provider offers and what care is and is not available. Will they, or can they provide Hospice care? Wound care? Care for insulin-dependent clients? Will they provide night care with awake-night staff, or two-person transfers? I'll cover more on these services later, but for now, remember that you want to have these questions answered before you move your loved one anywhere!

It's also very common for a non-nurse adult family home provider to coordinate skilled oversight with Visiting Nurse Services, Occupational Therapy, Physical Therapy, or Hospice Care providers. Mental Health Therapy can also be brought into the home when indicated. If these kinds of care are not mentioned, be sure to ask.

Specialty Licenses in Adult Family Homes

Washington has three specialty certifications, which are noted on the provider's license:

- Mental Health
- Dementia
- Developmental Disabilities

If a resident has a diagnosis of dementia, for example, he or she can only be admitted to a home that has a dementia specialty. The same goes for other diagnoses and specialties.

How Are Adult Family Homes Regulated?

Not so long ago, the Seattle Times declared Adult Family Homes to be "poorly regulated mom-and-pop operations." Although the "mom and pop" aspect is what made AFHs popular to begin with, that statement is far from the truth today, and is in fact quite misleading.

Washington State has one of the most stringent licensing requirements in the nation, ensuring that our seniors receive excellent care in a safe environment.

Adult Family Home providers must be licensed by the Department of Social Health Services (DSHS) and must adhere to strict rules and regulations found in WAC (Washington Administrative Code) 388-76, WAC 388-112, and other RCWs (Revised Code of Washington).

When you think that Adult Families Home have a capacity limit of just six residents, compared to hundreds of residents in Nursing Homes, the regulatory burden is significant.

> *In fact, Nursing Homes have 92% more residents on average, but only 12% more regulations. So if anyone tells you Adult Family Homes are a poorly regulated industry, now you know better!*

DSHS issues only one license per provider/operator and per home. Licensed homes/providers are inspected by DSHS licensors on a 12-month cycle average. Inspections occur without notice and the licensee must be in compliance at all times.

I've also heard the argument that because residential care settings are somewhat less supervised, there is a tendency to slack off on observing regulations. It used to be that the fines and penalties were minimal, such as $100 per violation. But today, many violations do incur fines of up to $1000 per day, for each day that the violation or deficiency remains present or uncorrected. With fines such as these, there is enormous pressure to comply with the laws and "slacking off" can have devastating consequences for a care provider.

The vast majority of providers strive to obey laws and provide high quality care; their livelihoods depend on it and the stakes are high.

Debunking the Poor Educational Requirements Myth

Contrary to what the press will have you believe, not "just anyone off the street" can easily get a license to care for frail seniors—it hasn't been the case for many years. As you can see below, adult family care homes (at least in Washington State) have significant educational requirements, which keep all but the most serious people from ever becoming care providers.

Education & Certification Requirements (2013)

1. DSHS Orientation class about becoming a provider (8 hrs.)
2. High School Diploma
3. 1000 hours of documented supervised care
4. Orientation & Safety Course (5 hrs.)
5. First Aid certification (4 hrs.)
6. CPR certification (4 hrs.)
7. Food Handler's permit (1 hr.)
8. Aids & HIV training (7 hrs.)
9. AFH Administration & Business Planning Course (52 hrs.)
10. Home Care Aid Certification (75 hrs.)
11. Nurse Delegation Course (10 hrs.)
12. 12 hours of Continuing Education Yearly
13. Specialty Training in Dementia Care (8-12 hrs.)
14. Specialty Training in Mental Health (8-12 hrs.)
15. Specialty Training in Developmental Disability (8-12 hrs.)
16. TB testing
17. Criminal Background check with FBI fingerprinting

In addition to these training requirements, the State Patrol Criminal Background check must be redone every two years, and many of these certifications have expiration dates and must be renewed accordingly.

To obtain a license, providers must also...

- Pay a Non-Refundable License Application Fee of $2,750
- Pay a Yearly License Renewal Fee of $225, per Bed—and rising.

In comparison, Nursing Homes usually employ Certified Nursing Assistants (NA-C) to provide the hands-on care to residents, which only require about 80 hours of total training. Since adult family home providers often deliver the primary hands-on care themselves, you will be in good hands.

For such a small business, these extensive requirements create a substantial barrier to entry to the industry and keep the growth rate quite modest, especially when compared to assisted living facilities.

The process to start a new Adult Family Home requires a significant financial and time investment—without any guarantee of being issued a license.

Long-Term Care Ombudsman Program

Another program that aids in ensuring quality care for our seniors is the State's Long-Term Care Ombudsman Program.

The Ombudsman Program exists in all states under the authorization of the Older Americans Act. Each state has an Office of the State Long-Term Care Ombudsman, directed by a full-time state ombudsman. Thousands of local ombudsman staff and volunteers visit adult family homes and other care facilities throughout the country as part of the statewide ombudsman programs, assisting and providing a voice for those unable to speak for themselves.

The law grants them access to records, staff, residents, and family members. They come unannounced, offering an additional level of monitoring and safety.

Is an Adult Family Home the Right Choice for My Parent or Loved One?

Just a few days ago I checked-in with one of my newer client's daughter, Susie. Her 82-year-old mother, Pat, moved in to one of my care homes two weeks ago, and the positive changes that Susie noted about her mom's adjustments were immediate and substantial; "I haven't seen mom up and dressed for months. She's interacting with the other residents and seems a lot more engaged in life.
She was so isolated at home, had nothing to live for, and mainly stayed in her pajamas."

On a daily basis, any of Pat's five children and more grandkids than I can keep track of stop by for a visit. They love seeing how well has Pat adjusted to her new home and have found a new, positive way to contribute to Pat's life – without the burden of personal care. As for Pat, receiving "loved visitors" is a powerful reason to get out of bed, get dressed, and is something worth living for!

Caring for your loved one does not have to be a solo act; let it be a partnership. For so many, the thought of meeting every one of your parent's needs, managing your own life, and the myriad other obligations is overwhelming.

Embracing the idea of getting a care provider's help will not only mean the more skilled care and safety your parent deserves, it will often redefine your role in their life, and allow you to re-create balance in *your* life. Isn't that something your parent would want?

A good Adult Family Home can deliver the most competent and nurturing care available, especially in Washington State. In general, if your loved one needs "custodial care," that is, personal care and assistance with activities of daily living (aka ADLs) like dressing, bathing, medication assistance, supervision, and the like, an Adult Family Home is an ideal choice for many reasons.

If your loved one has memory impairment or any level of confusion or dementia, an Adult Family Home becomes an even better choice, with a few exceptions.

In the following chapters, we'll explore some of the issues that lead to considering a move. Often times these arise because of concerns for a loved one's safety, quality of life, health decline, or accident.

How do we recognize safety issues in our parent's current living arrangement? And when we do, how do we talk with them about moving? Each family's circumstance is obviously different so let's find out how to assess the level of risk in their current living situation.

Memory Care Units for Seniors With Dementia

Should you avoid institutional Memory Care Units if your parent has dementia?

Before going further, let's define the term 'memory care units' as it is used in today's long-term-care environment.

Memory care is a distinct form of specialized long-term care that specifically caters to people with Alzheimer's disease, dementia, and other types of memory problems. Memory care units provide 24-hour supervised care in a separate wing or floor of a residential facility. The physical layout and security of memory care unit is designed to better suit Alzheimer's and dementia patients, and to minimize the negative impact of wandering behavior. For example, there is no easy way for a resident to wander off onto the street, or outside the locked unit.

Although the term 'memory care unit' is typically associated with larger, more institutional assisted-living facilities, a majority of adult family homes do possess a dementia specialty license and offer excellent – and more personalized – care for seniors with Alzheimer's disease and dementia.

Let's look at the pros and cons.

Considerations *in Favor* of Institutional Memory Care Units:

- Highly challenging behaviors can more easily be managed in larger settings that are accustomed to it and the additional staff makes that job easier.
- Nursing and support staff is highly trained and is used to managing challenging behaviors.
- You don't have to worry about your loved one fitting-in or disturbing others.

Considerations *Against* Institutional Memory Care Units:

- Generally, an institutional memory care environment is highly taxing to a person with dementia. The environment is often too stimulating for a brain that cannot process sensory input and information normally.

- The lights are on 24/7, further inhibiting the pineal gland's ability to produce melatonin, a hormone that induces sleep and restoration.
- Too many people and caregivers overwhelm the brain's ability to process stimuli, causing more stress and precipitating more challenging behaviors.
- The continual change in staffing and residents make establishing routines and forming relationships more difficult.
- Residents are behind closed doors when they are in their own quarters, leading to less supervision and more accidents.

Is the Adult Family Home environment better for those with dementia or memory impairment?

Generally, yes, in my view, and here's why:

- The smaller and calmer environment requires less brain processing power, and therefore causes less stress and triggers fewer difficult behaviors.
- There is more personal attention and redirection available whenever necessary.
- Since it's a much smaller setting, a greater sense of familiarity with fewer staff and surroundings help decrease stress and "catastrophic events." Catastrophic events are emotional outbursts and overreactions to seemingly normal, non-threatening situations. Sometimes these reactions are accompanied by physical acting-out. The word catastrophic implies that there is a catastrophe, or a that a terrible event occurred, but that is usually not the case; *catastrophic* is the way it feels to the person experiencing the event. These catastrophic events can be triggered by such things as too much noise, recalling stressful memories, trying to provide personal care, or unnecessary changes in the environment such as staffing changes.

Caution: If your loved one has a propensity to leave the premises to "go home" or wander off outside the home, you should make sure the Adult Family Home has a secured perimeter and is well-staffed to manage these attempts.

When is an Adult Family Home Not the Best Choice for Dementia or Memory Impaired Patients?

- If your loved one has highly challenging behaviors such as aggressive, disruptive, or sexually inappropriate tendencies.
- If he/she is very socially active, needs the company of others in staying busy, or likes many outings.
- If they like and need many stimulating activities on a daily basis.

Some Adult Family Homes do offer this level of stimulation. But in general, some residents who require lots of activity may feel bored and more isolated in an Adult Family Home. For these more active folks, an assisted living facility may be a better setting, where the levels of activity and socialization are much higher.

Is it Time to Move into a Care Facility?

How do you know when that time has come?

Sometime you just do. Other times, you get caught thinking the hardship may soon pass and you should just hold tight… but the struggle continues on.

As you care for your life partner, sibling, or a loved one, you may have uneasy feelings as you watch them physically and/or mentally decline.

Then, just as you get ready to talk about moving into an Adult Family Home where she can receive the care she needs, out of nowhere she'll say, "I don't want to move." Your stomach knots... she was always something of a mind reader!

Seniors who need additional care are often reluctant to confess their changing needs for fear of losing their home, possessions, and independence. At the same time, family members often suffer from their own emotional loss, denial, and differing opinions on how to proceed, creating an even more challenging situation. No matter what the circumstances—fear, discomfort, and inaction can leave you unprepared if a crisis occurs.

Here is a typical scenario: you drop in to visit your mom at her Assisted Living Facility, only to find her unit in a mess; the refrigerator is full of spoiled food and she's still in her pajamas – at 3:30 in the afternoon.

You've known for a while that she has progressed to an age where she'll soon need more help, but you just haven't had the heart to bring it up. It's difficult for everyone. You're wondering what this means for her, and what it will mean for you. How will she react as you broach the subject of the inevitable limitations that her declining health is bringing?

Knowing IF it's the right time to move is a big challenge in itself. You sense that things aren't right, yet you feel torn; is it only in your mind or is she really at serious risk of harm?

You can answer this question by reading "5 Key Questions to Ask to Determine Whether a Move to a Care Facility is a Good Idea."

There are typically two ways in which a move will occur:

The Accident

A person will sustain a fall, an injury, or health issue such as dehydration. They're taken to a local hospital, and told they can't go back home. All too often, this is the only way adult children finally get their parent to greater safety.

The obvious drawback to this sequence of events is that everything is rushed resulting in fewer choices, a lot more stress, and invariably more expense. As the adult child or Power of Attorney, you have no choice on the timing and will be forced to take action whether or not you have the time, support, or know-how.

The Anticipated, Planned Move

In this case, you can tell the situation is precarious and proceed to clearly assess present risks. Then you educate yourself on possible options (i.e. by reading this book) so you are able to make a clearer and more informed decision in the best interest of your parent. You are able to plan and execute a move on your terms, and on your time.

Making the decision to move an elderly parent is never easy, especially when the elder lives in his or her own home. That being said, after the move most people feel relieved and experience less stress...and that includes you!

Jack's Story

In 2009, I met Jack, a lovely 82-year-old man with severe emphysema. Jack's daughter, Joyce, who resided out-of-state, reached out to me after a visit with her father who still lived alone in his own home.

Even though at first sight Jack seemed to be getting along okay, she became worried about him based on her some concerning observations. This led her to feel that more serious problems would invariably arise unless she took action. Joyce listened to her instinct.

Jack was on oxygen supplementation and loved smoking cigars inside the house, with all blinds and windows completely shut—a potentially deadly combination. The home was in serious disrepair and needed extensive maintenance. Jack had lost significant weight due to malnutrition, and was also dehydrated. There was spoiled food just about everywhere she looked.

He was isolated and had become socially withdrawn from friends and family, and he was depressed. He couldn't manage his medications safely and no one could tell which drugs were actively prescribed, or expired. Jack was weak, could barely walk, and had sustained several falls. The list of concerns went on.

Ultimately Joyce decided it was a smarter idea to act before disaster struck.

After due diligence, Jack moved into one of my care homes and his life literally transformed for the better. He delighted in the company of another man and four women.

When we discovered that Jack had played the piano in the past, we encouraged him to sit at our baby grand and see what happened. One day, he finally did and to our amazement, Jack happened to be a master at the piano! He instantly grew an audience and every day after lunch he delighted our senses with beautiful music. Doing so restored a powerful sense of contribution and meaning to his life.

We established a safe smoking area under a covered patio where Jack could continue to [safely] enjoying his cigars, something he was not ready to give up. Joyce told me that she couldn't remember ever seeing her dad so happy.

5 Key Areas to Determine if a Move to a Care Facility is a Good Idea

Answering "yes" to some of the questions below does not necessarily mean your loved one must be relocated. However, if many of your answers *are* "yes," then it is possible that having your loved one remain at home is no longer a safe and viable option.

1. Mobility Issues

- Have there been falls? A fall resulting in an injury almost always results in a decreased quality of life.
- Can your loved one move safely about the house? Are there stairs to negotiate? Can she get in and out of the bathroom safely?
- Does your loved one have and use necessary safety equipment and mobility aids? Can they use personal emergency devices?

2. General Safety Issues

- Have accidents occurred recently with appliances, such as leaving the stove on?
- If your loved one smokes, do you see burn holes in clothing or bedding?
- In the event of a fire, do you feel they could call 911 and evacuate the house safely?
- If your loved one uses oxygen, are there potential dangers related to smoking or open flames (such as stoves)?
- Has your loved one gotten lost or been unable to remember his address, phone number, or important contacts?

3. Health Issues

- Medications: do you find prescription bottles full? Or un-emptied medication organizers?
- Do you feel a need to call personally and ask, "Have you taken your blood pressure medication today?" Are they able to follow the correct dosage?
- Are they receiving proper nutrition? Do you find rotten food in the fridge? Do you find yourself preparing food, only to find it

untouched upon your next visit?

- Has a recent medical visit revealed dehydration or other metabolic imbalances?
- Have they suffered recent weight loss, or has refusing to eat become a problem?
- Is your loved unable to maintain adequate hygiene (including hair, clothing, oral, and incontinent care)?
- Have they become progressively more dependent on you for help with eating, dressing, or bathing?
- Is it difficult for them to allow outside help when needed (for personal care, housekeeping chores, or meal preparation)?

4. Care Management Issues

1. Are you able to find qualified help to relieve you of some of your caregiving responsibilities?
2. Have they become unreasonably paranoid, fearful, or suspicious of others, of taking medications, or of eating certain foods?
3. Are your caregiver duties causing you to be sleep deprived, anxious, miss work, or be unable to manage your own responsibilities?
4. Is your loved one willing to participate in an adult day care program to relieve some of your caregiving responsibilities?
5. **Do you personally have enough support? Do you feel resentful, burdened, or depressed?**

5. Financial Consideration Issues

1. Is the amount of care needed becoming so great that it's no longer an affordable option?
2. Do you find unnecessary or unopened products ordered from TV commercials and magazine ads?
3. Did you find multiple new credit cards or a surprising drop in savings?

Answering these questions honestly is a great step toward taking action on your loved one's behalf. We know it's difficult, so we've provided you with tips that will help you get off to a strong start. Talking about the change of living needs is challenging, and the unknown is the scariest part for both you and your loved one.

8 Tips for Discussing Change of Living Situation with Your Loved One

Such conversations are challenging and stressful, but these simple guidelines, even if they don't seem earth-shattering, can make a big difference.

1. You might begin by having a conversation with someone she respects, such as her doctor or clergyman. Express your concerns regarding her current mental, physical, and emotional condition, and arrange a meeting. Discussing the necessity for change may be easier for her to hear from a professional and may help take the heat off of you, lending credibility to your future conversations.

2. Set aside and schedule plenty of time when everyone is rested and prepared. Do not rush this conversation.

3. Keep the group as small as possible. Only the key players should attend to avoid your loved one feeling overwhelmed or ganged-up on.

4. Allow each person to talk without interruptions or criticism – listen to learn. It's critical that everyone feels heard and is able to express his or her thoughts. Often times, having the ability to simply voice resentments, anger, or fears goes a long way in dissipating those unpleasant feelings.

5. Understand that emotions may run high. Be patient, it may take some time to get things out on the table and to find resolutions to everyone's concerns.

6. Stay positive, but realistic.

7. Your elderly parent or loved one should have a central role in determining what is needed and how it is accomplished, unless an impaired cognitive state or dementia problems prevent it. If your loved one can voice a clear opinion, take it into consideration. You can also bring them along when touring care homes, but only AFTER you've pre-screened them and narrowed the choices down to just 2 or 3 maximum. If their judgment is impaired, you are better off making that choice

yourself, perhaps with other siblings.

8. Allow time for everyone to think about what was discussed. Remember to consider whether you are in a position to make recommendations rather than decisions. For instance, if you have the Power of Attorney for Health Care for someone with dementia, this will be very different than if the conversation involves a fully cognizant person.

Remember: it normally takes more than one conversation to make a plan and even small, consistent steps will yield positive outcomes. Try not to tackle too many issues at once.

You Have Decided it is Time for a Move: Next Steps

Before you start your search for a placement, collect the facts about your loved one's needs.

Make a long-term care assessment and get clear on needs. Get clear on your love one's actual needs including physical limitations, safety needs, cognitive status, as well as the overall medical acuity ("acuity" is the overall complexity of medical issues). In other words, how complicated are their medical needs?

You can hire a professional or use our <u>Easy Senior Care Assessment</u> form. This will assist you when calling or touring facilities.

Decide which type of facility is best for you. As soon as you're clear on needs, choosing a type of facility is your next step. If you feel like it's a toss-up between two kinds, you can get a better sense of what it's like to live in each by simply visiting. Try visualizing your loved one living there and how that setting may meet his/her present *and* future needs.

Get a list of facilities. Go to your state's website and get a list based on location and type. For Washington State follow these links:

- <u>Adult Family Homes</u> (https://fortress.wa.gov/dshs/adsaapps/lookup/AFHAdvLookup.asp
- <u>Assisted Living Facilities</u> (licensed)
- You can also use <u>Adult Family Homes Central</u>

Make Preliminary Calls. Once care needs and preferences are clarified, and you have a list of basic questions to ask, make your calls and set up touring appointments as appropriate.

Take action and follow through. I find over and over again that those who don't act usually go through needless traumatic events including costly and stressful hospitalizations. At that point, your options become reduced and more costly.

Keep the assessment handy and use it while interviewing potential facilities.

How to Determine Your Loved One's Level of Care Needs

OK, you've concluded that it is time—maybe past time—to help your loved one into a care facility. You're ready to begin your search for just the right "Home".

You're armed with a list of questions and before you can even start firing, you're being bombarded with questions, questions, and more questions. What's more, they're often questions you can't answer.

Take heart, it doesn't have to be so difficult. What you need are some answers, and I'm here to help.
Understanding your parent's care needs is imperative to finding the right facility and appropriate care for him or her. A Long Term Care Assessment is simply a more detailed evaluation to help you get clear on your loved one's actual needs.

Of course, there are various levels of depth and focus to these assessments, and this section only discusses long-term care assessments relative to custodial geriatric care (meaning non-acute and non-medical care).

For the purpose of searching for care facilities, follow this link to a simplified assessment:
(http://www.spadahomes.com/downloads/Level-of-care-assessment_v2.pdf)

For the purpose of searching for care facilities, follow this link to a simplified assessment:
(http://www.spadahomes.com/downloads/Level-of-care-assessment_v2.pdf)Once you've answered and documented the basic questions above, take it a step further and ask **"How are these needs likely to progress?"**

You want to know HOW your loved one's needs are likely to change so you can plan ahead, making sure the potential facility would be able to meet them if necessary. (See the chapter on *"How to Avoid Moving Again Due to Unanticipated Future Needs."*)

Too many people make the mistake of choosing a care facility based on current needs without thinking about future needs. By considering future needs, you could avoid another move. I am going to show you how to determine potential future needs to help you avoid an unnecessary move in the event your loved one needs more care in the future.

10 Key Considerations When Looking for Senior Care

Here is a quick list of important points when evaluating a care facility of any kind.

1. Convenient location! Make sure the location is convenient to your home or work; otherwise it will quickly become a burden to visit and manage.
2. Quality care that meets your loved one's medical and emotional needs, both now and in the future.
3. Ability of the care provider to meet future needs, and provide end-of-life care.
4. Safe and clean environment. This means adequate staff day and night; no area rugs; no clutter; no steps; handrails; enough grab-bars; etc.
5. Caring, respectful, and compassionate staff with the ability to communicate effectively.
6. Relaxed atmosphere and clear communication with owner and staff.
7. Able to meet your loved one's social interests.
8. Welcomes and encourages family and friends visits and participation.
9. Compatible with current and anticipated future financial resources.
10. Citations and Enforcement Letters-free home (more on this later).

How to Avoid Having to Move Again Due to Unanticipated Future Needs

I suggest that you go through this exercise with me; it could potentially save you a lot of time and precious resources.

Take a piece of paper and your favorite pen, and then draw a line down the middle of the page, from top to bottom. On the left-hand side, write down every medical diagnosis and health problem your loved one has currently. Include things like "overweight" or "diabetic."

On the right-hand side, write down all of the possible anticipated needs that might arise based on the typical disease progression for each issue on the left. This is NOT the time to think best-case scenario. Think of the old adage "hope for the best, prepare for the worst." You want to think about possible tough times ahead… if the toughest issues come up, what problems might you be dealing with?

Anticipation of Future Needs

Your loved one may be stable now, but consider their future needs. Here are a few examples of future needs based on a person's current health issues:

- **Emphysema** – may later need help with…

  - Help with oxygen use
  - Help walking due to shortness of breath
  - Help with nebulizers and other inhalers
  - Chair lift for stairs

- **Diabetes** – may later need help with…

  - Injections, including sliding scale "as-needed" injections
  - Blood glucose monitoring checks
  - Special diet
  - Wound care & non-healing skin sores
  - Blindness

- **Alzheimer's** disease – may later need help with…

- May wander or elope off the property (elope means leaving or escaping)
- May become agitated, even aggressive
- May refuse care
- May have repetitive difficult behaviors
- May develop inappropriate toileting habits
- May be very active at night

As you search for the right care home or facility, keep your loved one's *future needs* in mind. Ask all potential care providers how they may deal with specific issues that you may have identified above.

For example, if your loved one has dementia, ask the potential providers, "how would you handle it if my mom refused personal care after soiling herself?" Or, "what if she becomes sleepless at night, or wanders into other people's bedrooms?" Be as specific as possible with the anticipated challenging need.

Aging in Place

If you've spent much time researching long-term care options, you're probably aware the industry has a language all its own, chock-full of mysterious terms, abbreviations and axioms, including "aging in place." What does that *really* mean, and how important is it as you make life and housing plans for your parents—or for that matter, yourself?!

> ***Aging-in-place defined:*** *In general, "aging in place" means having the ability to live in your own home, community, or care home safely and comfortably, regardless of age, income, or level of ability.*

As your health declines and your personal and medical needs increase, you would remain in the familiar setting that you currently call "home" and with a familiar support system to care for you.

Your care needs would be met safely, adequately, and comfortably without being displaced, and eventually you would receive the support and expertise of Hospice care services.

Personalize YOUR Definition for Aging in Place

I encourage you to further refine this definition for yourself. For example, many large facilities will tell you they offer aging in place, and what they mean is this: you'll stay with the same organization and in the same campus, but you'll be moved to a different floor or wing with different surroundings, people and staff. Do you buy into that definition?

7 Reasons Why Adult Family Homes in Washington State are a Great Setting for "Aging in Place" and Should be Considered when Choosing a Long-Term Care Setting

The following reasons are some of the greatest benefits of adult family homes in Washington.

1. The staff skill level is high due to state-mandated training and licensing requirements. Washington State has some of the most stringent requirements in the nation for providers and staff.

2. Hospice care, visiting nurses, physical therapists, and in-home doctors can all be coordinated to provide professional services and oversight in the adult family home.

3. The Adult Family Home deals with staffing needs, so you don't have to. The staff is familiar and typically a lot more consistent than in larger facilities.

4. No need to move to another room, wing, unit, or location – you're home!

5. Generally more flexible and supportive of families' and friends' presence and care-giving efforts.

6. More likely to be prepared for end of life care than assisted living, and less clinical than other options such as Nursing Homes, or in the event of an emergency, hospitals.

7. According to some estimates from the University of Washington, residents in adult family homes receive, on average, 60% more hands-on care than they do in assisted living facilities.

Limitations of Care: Who is Not a Good Fit for an Adult Family Home?

Because Adult Family Homes are small settings, residents who are noisy, disruptive, or aggressive may not be appropriate there, but some providers may be able to accommodate them if they specialize in this type of care. "Specializing in this type of care" means that the other residents in the home have similar issues and needs, and that provider's primary focus is to provide care for such residents.

Additionally, if a resident poses a safety risk to self or others, I would not recommend the AFH setting.

Generally speaking, residents in Adult Family Homes should be in stable and predictable medical condition. Residents with more complex medical issues should be admitted to homes owned and operated by RN or LPN providers who have the necessary training, experience, and staff to deal with more acute and complicated medical issues.

If a resident is experiencing a more acute illness such as delirium, an infection requiring IV treatment, or is medically unstable for any reason, you should consider a medical or nursing home stay prior to moving into an adult family home. Once medically stable you can move forward with an AFH placement. If an acute medical condition returns after the adult family home placement, the resident would likely need another hospital stay. Note that this will be the case even in a nursing home facility where residents are frequently sent to hospitals in case of acute medical conditions.

How to Search for and Find Adult Family Homes

You're working, you're caring for yourself and your family, and you're now caring for your aging parent as well, which may include doctor appointments, banking, special dietary needs, shopping, dressing, and bathing. Perhaps you oversee around-the-clock caregivers, or worse, you do it all yourself!

Your parent is unhappy and/or is in failing health, you're tired and stressed out, and **YOU NEED HELP!**

By now you may have completed the *Easy Senior Care Assessment* (if not, go HERE). With that, you're ready to take your next step in this process: finding a partner—a good care facility.

In general, you have two options for finding an Adult Family Home or facility: do it yourself or seek help through a referral agent. But before you seek the assistance of a referral agency, I strongly encourage you read the section on working with referral agents.

1. Let's begin with some options for doing it yourself.
   * Go to the Adult Family Homes Central website, search page. Alternately, go to the DSHS website (for Washington state).

Adult Family Homes (AFHs) Central will help you locate and connect you to care providers directly—it's a free service. Because we focus on Adult Family Homes exclusively, you can find a good match through our listing of state-licensed Adult Family Homes in the State of Washington.
Here is what you'll find:

* A direct link between you and Adult Family Home providers in Washington State – no middleman.
* Education – relevant articles on long-term care.
* Assessment Tools – you'll determine when your loved one needs care and what level of care they need.
* Support through an online forum and blog.
* All services are FREE.
* Care providers don't pay any referral fees (that's very important

for you!)

- Adult Family Homes Central will never benefit from your choice of provider. (No conflict of interest.)

2. Word-of-mouth can go a long way: You've all heard the story—the best advertising is word of mouth. People like to talk and whether they've had a good experience or bad, they want to tell their story.

Do you know someone who has been an advocate or caregiver for an older adult, or someone who knows someone who has? They can be a wealth of information, but be careful about taking advice... look for the kernel of information that may be helpful to you in your research then check it out for yourself. NO BLIND TRUST!

3. Geriatric Professionals: Geriatricians and geriatric care managers can be an excellent resource, to a certain point. As your loved one's physician, they may assist you in determining the level of care needed, what type of facility to consider and they may even recommend a facility or two to help you get started.

And finally, once you've compiled a list of facilities, pick up the telephone and start making calls! The following questions will help you make quick progress and save time by getting right to the point – just fill-in the blanks.

Ask these 3 simple questions for a quick start:

1. Do you have beds available? (Ask for "Medicaid beds" if applicable).
2. Can you provide care for my [AGE] year old [MOTHER'S/FATHER] who has [SPECIFIC MEDICAL CONDITION]? With your Easy Care Senior Assessment in hand, you are now prepared to briefly discuss off your loved one's care needs.
3. When can I visit? If you received positive responses to questions 1 and 2, make an appointment to tour the facility.

IMPORTANT: before you go for a visit, check the State's website for enforcement letters or licensing issues. Read THIS CHAPTER for details on enforcement letters.

Once you've gotten a list of Adult Family Homes you feel may be a match, you're almost ready to start touring.

Touring Adult Family Homes – Part 1

Staying Out of Overwhelm

Overwhelm is an issue that often gets in the way of effectively dealing with a frail aging parent and navigating the care options. I want to suggest a couple ideas to help you minimize that.

The following sections on touring adult family homes (and care facilities in general) are quite extensive; *you do not need to learn and memorize everything in them!*

The idea is to quickly go over and review the topics and questions I suggest and pick the most relevant to you—then go with those. For example, a provider's pet policy may not be relevant to your case, unless your parent wants to bring his pet, or is allergic to dog dander.

To help you discern what questions or topics are most important I use an asterisks * just before those items.

Feel free to write down some of the questions and take them with you.

Considerations when Touring and Selecting an AFH

For many folks this is a journey into uncharted territory, and there is a lot to consider as you tour Adult Family Homes.

The most important factors are comfort, reliability and trust, quality of care, and safety. As you're heading out the door with your list of homes to tour, let me help you focus on what to look for, what questions to ask, and how to recognize the right answers when you hear them.

This chapter guides you step-by-step through the touring process. Part 1 contains important considerations and things for you to keep in mind. In Part 2, I've compiled a list of relevant interview questions and things to talk about with a potential care provider. Finally, in Part 3, you'll find even more particulars to help you leave no stone unturned – ideal if you are detail-oriented!

Top 7 Considerations

1. **Skill Level and Future Care**

    - The owners' and staffs' care credentials and education should meet industry and state standards. (See How Are Adult Family Homes Regulated?**)**

    - The facility should be able to provide the level of care that your loved one needs currently and in the future as their care needs progress.

    - Is the provider prepared to manage a client with higher care needs if necessary? Can your loved one "age in place" with Hospice care?

    - Care Plan: ideally, the care plan must be personalized and tailored to the resident's needs, not boilerplate language, and not designed to accommodate the home's routine.

    - Clear procedures for managing and distributing medications should be in place. A good Adult Family Home provider has quality systems above and beyond the minimum state requirements. Ask the provider to explain the medication management system and procedures in place to get a feel for their organization.

    - To check a provider's skill level you can ask him/her, "How would you handle [INSERT CARE CHALLENGE HERE]." For example, "How would you handle it if Mom refused her medication?"

2. **Home Composition and Resident Mix**

    - Ensuring a good match with the other residents in the homes is very important. For example, if your mom is conversational, find a home where the other residents are also conversational. Most importantly, try to avoid the cross dementia/non-dementia fit, where your loved one is the only person that is not demented, or the only one with dementia when everyone is alert and oriented.

- Try to find an environment where new relationships can flourish. For instance, if the current residents all share meals together at the dining table, it will foster more socialization opportunities.
- Staff's ability to interact and connect with your loved one. This is very important, because other residents may be unable to interact well. For example, many are hard of hearing or sight-impaired, making communication more difficult. If the staff are shy, withdrawn, or have poor communication skills, your loved one may experience more isolation.

3. Finances

- **Cost of Care.** If you're interested in a home and provider, ask for a price range. If that figure falls within your budget, make arrangements to provide them with more information about care needs (Your Easy Senior Care Assessment will work great for this), and ask for a specific price. After the provider has ascertained the care level required, they should be able to provide a firm price.

    a)   If a provider simply quotes a price without doing their due diligence, they may come back later saying your loved one requires more care than previously thought and try to increase the care fee.

- **Care Fee**. Adult Family Homes may use a monthly fee or a daily rate based on room selection, board, and level of care needs. Ask if care needs are broken out and calculated separately or as a flat rate.

    a)   Be sure to discuss when and how fee increases may come into effect, as well as additional fees for services you'll need to pay.

- **Move-in Fees or Security Deposits**. Plan for at least $325-$400 to pay for the initial DSHS Long-Term Care Assessment, and $200 to $300 annually thereafter for assessment updates. These are required in Washington and usually done by independent RNs who are "qualified assessors" for state in which they reside. Some providers, especially RNs, will sometime provide these at no cost to you.

- **Refund Policy**. What if your loved one moves out within the first month? Or after that…what are the refund policies?

- **Very Low Prices** that are well below market rates may signal low-paid staff, reduced staffing, no night staff, lower quality of food, or fewer services or activities. If that's the case, you might ask what gives them the ability to offer lower-than-average prices.

- **Medicaid Policy**. What is the policy for accepting Medicaid or transferring to Medicaid payment at a later date? Is there a minimum stay before they accept Medicaid? Will your loved one have to change rooms or location?

4. **Safety & Security**

- * How well does the staff speak English? Staff should be able to communicate clearly with residents, family, and 911 if there is an accident or emergency.

- The building should be furnished and laid out with the residents' ease and safety in mind. Floor plans and furniture should be easy to navigate.

- Safety equipment such as handrails, raised toilet seats, and sit down shower benches should be installed.

- What are the procedures to prevent a wandering client from leaving the home? Some care homes offer a secured perimeter, where a confused client may wonder outside the house, but not leave the facility grounds.

- Is there a call system for residents to call for help?

5. **Location & Convenience**

- No matter how good an Adult Family Home or long-term care facility is, your job does not end after move-in. I strongly suggest you plan to remain actively involved in your loved one's care, and knowing that you can stop by whenever you may be worried contributes to peace of mind. With this in mind, consider the following:

- Start by selecting care homes closest to your home or work. The location should be easily accessible.

- Try to be near the hospital where your loved one has received care, or near the hospital his/her primary care physician is associated with (although nowadays, most hospitals use "hospitalists" until the patient is released back to the primary care doctor after hospitalization).

6. **Licensing, State Encumbrances, References**

- The care home or facility should be properly licensed by the state, and be free from licensing encumbrances or enforcement letters.

- Washington State has 3 specialty certifications, which are noted on the provider's license: Mental Health Specialty, Dementia Specialty, and Developmental Disabilities Specialty. If your loved one has a diagnosis of dementia, the care provider must also have a dementia specialty license prior to providing care or else they'll receive a citation from the state.

- * The DSHS license must be posted on a wall and readily visible by visitors. This is also true for State inspection reports. If the facility has an encumbrance on their license, the State issues a new license stating the facility has an encumbered status, and that new license must be posted and visible. I suggest you actually look at the license and read it.

- Enforcement Letters. For more information on enforcement letters see the section below about enforcement letters and how to check if a care facility has one.

7. **State Surveys**

No matter what type of long-term care facility you are looking for, you can view a copy of their annual State Survey. These are generally posted someplace obvious such as near the entryway, near the phone or where the State license is posted. After their annual State Survey, facilities are required to develop a "plan of correction" to address any deficiencies, and to make those surveys available to you.

The simplest way to deal with State Inspections Surveys is to ask, "Can I see your last State survey?" Once in-hand, THEN ask "do you have enforcement letters?" Ideally you need to check for enforcement letters on the State's website before your visit – it takes 5 minutes and anyone can do it.

To see if the home has an enforcement letter, read THIS Chapter.

Equipped with the information above, you can make an informed choice from a place of confidence. I know it's a big decision to make, but trust your instincts and if you have the luxury, take your time.

One more tip: surround yourself with support. Ask a friend, or another family member to accompany you as you tour… two hearts and two sets of eyes and ears are always better than one.

Touring Adult Family Homes – Part 2

Field Questionnaire

Let's shift gears to focus on the Adult Family Home provider and staff. They will have daily contact with your loved one, and will essentially become partners in care and the residents' extended family.

For that reason, you want to like them, and more importantly, to trust them. Communication should be open and smooth. The owner's philosophy and values are reflected throughout the home, policies, and systems. Simply paying attention during your visit will give you valuable insights. Based on what you see, do they value cleanliness, attention to detail, and organization?

Let's begin with what to look for in the owner of an Adult Family Home. He or she sets the tone and quality standards for the home through their skill level, knowledge, and experience. In any care setting, your overall feeling about the provider or administrator is the best indicator of all, along with his/her background, experience, and motivation for doing this work.

Owner/Provider/Administrator Skill Level and Experience

- The provider should have some level of nursing education and experience in geriatrics; preferably a RN or LPN who works in and oversees the daily business of their Adult Family Home.
- If the provider has nursing education and experience, what's their level of involvement in the day-to-day operation? Do they maintain a job outside the care home? This is important, because if they do, then they may not actually be available when needed.
- Ask what nursing care services they are personally able – or willing – to provide.
- Have they cared for residents with similar diagnoses or challenges?
- Keep in mind that some Certified Nursing Assistants have excellent skills as well, albeit without the deeper and more technical nursing background and understanding.

TIP: A good casual way to check for relevant skills is to ask questions such as, "If Dad started yelling at your staff, how would you handle it?" Make sure the questions are relevant to your parent's specific medical condition.

Geriatric Care Certification

The Geriatric Care Certification is a newer program offered through the University of Washington's Geriatric Education Center (UW School of Nursing). This program is recognized by the Department of Social and Health Services (DSHS) and requires 52 credits (72 hours) of specific geriatric care education, with testing.

A certification is issued to the AFH licensee by DSHS. This is a high-quality program specifically geared to geriatric health promotion and includes more than 30 modules taught by physicians, PhDs, RN educators and social workers. This program is above and beyond the regular Adult Family Home minimum licensing requirements, so it reflects the value a provider places on higher levels of excellence, rather than simply meeting standards.

Questions for Owner/Operators

Basic Questions

- What is your schedule at the home?
- What is your motivation to own and/or operate an AFH?
- Is your home and staff guided by a particular philosophy or a mission statement?
- What does a typical day at the AFH look like?

Also, ask for a copy of the home's policies and for references from current clients and family members.

Questions About Administration and Staff

- Is there 24 hour AWAKE staffing? On-call staff during the night means the resident will have to call for help. This type of setting may be sufficient for some residents, but inadequate for residents who are incontinent or confused. If there is no awake night staff and your loved one needs more care in the future, how will the increased staffing needs affect your cost?
- How long has the staff worked there? What is the frequency of staff turnover?
- Is the staff nurse-delegated? That means an RN can delegate the non-licensed staff to perform routine nursing tasks for the resident

(such as blood sugar checks, medicated ointments, crushing medications, eye drops, etc.).

Care Schedule

1. Does the administration favor a firm schedule for providing personal care or is that flexible?
2. How many caregivers are on duty? Ask if and when there is two or more staff on duty. When the work is divided amongst several staff, the caregivers may be more alert and energetic. Also, they have more time for one-on-one interactions. Keep in mind that more staff means the staffing can be quickly changed as circumstances dictate, based on the overall care needs in the home.
3. **How long are the caregiver's shifts? Beware of one caregiver on duty 24 hours per day, unless ALL residents in the home are fairly independent and need only minimal care.**

Meals

1. What type of food do you serve? Are special requests granted? What about special diets? Food is important to seniors and oftentimes the highlight of their day!

2. Are the residents encouraged to eat at the same time, around the table? Or is everyone served at various times and/or in his or her own room?

3. Look at a menu if available, or ask what they typically cook. Share with the provider what your loved one likes to eat and ask if they can prepare it.

4. Better yet, visit at meal time – most providers should be happy to have you there.

Narrowing the Choices

When you have narrowed the field to your top 2-3 choices, take your loved one to lunch and tour each home—if they are able. Again, take your time if you can afford it. Talk with residents, staff, and family members if possible.

If your loved one is confused or has dementia, it may be wise to avoid bringing them along for a visit because it often adds stress for you both.

One critical ingredient is CONSISTENCY. It's easy to put on a good show during a tour, but what you want is consistent performance, not a one-time flash. The best way to see if the care, people, and routine are consistent is to make SEVERAL VISITS, and to stop by on short notice.

Touring Adult Family Homes – Part 3

More Touring Tips and Particulars

Can there possibly be more information to share regarding the touring of Adult Family Homes? YES! Here in the third and final installment on "How to Tour Adult Family Homes," I'll share some key details to help you make the best decision possible... let's call it the Nitty-Gritty.

You may find an item or two below to add to your interview list, as well as a few redundant ones... If you've read it more than once, it's because I feel it's worthy of the repeat.

Communication is Key.

If communication is difficult, even a small problem can become a huge challenge, especially over the long run. You can expect to work closely and communicate regularly with the owner of the home and the staff, possibly for years, so it's important that you feel comfortable.

General Interactions and Communication

- Pay attention to interactions between staff and residents. Are they talking? Smiling? Does the staff seem warm and caring, or tired and burned out?
- Notice English and communication skills. Many seniors have some impairment of hearing, vision, or speech. You are looking for providers and staff who are good communicators.

Silent Observations

- Be alert and trust your instincts. When you first enter a care home or facility, you'll notice interactions and objects you may not be accustomed to seeing. Take a moment to look and absorb the surroundings.
- Look for details like handrails and clean light switch plates.

Neighborhood & Outdoor Surroundings

- As you arrive, do you like the location and external appearance of the facility?

- Is there a garden or outside areas to sit, visit, or walk in?
- Is the facility on a noisy or busy street?
- * For dementia and clients who wander: is the exit door alarmed or is there a busy, dangerous street? Does the home offer a secured perimeter?
- Are there local amenities nearby to provide items your loved one may want?
- Is the location convenient for easy visits, either close to work, home, or in between?

Indoor Physical Setting

- Layout. Is the floor plan easy to follow? Long or confusing hallways can be quite disorienting to an elderly person.
- Disability Accommodations. Are doorways, hallways, and rooms accommodating to wheelchairs and walkers?
- Use of equipment your loved one may need:
- Mobility Devices. Does the facility have devices designed to aid individuals with mobility impairments, such as walkers, grab bars, and transfer poles?
- Durable Medical Equipment – Medical supplies and equipment such as hospital beds, oxygen tanks, raised toilet seats that would be used for a resident's care.
- Lighting: Is there ample natural and artificial lighting?
- Cleanliness: Does the house or facility meet your standard of cleanliness? Do you notice offensive odors? Use the bathroom. Is it clean?
- Hazards: Do you see excessive furnishings and tight spaces? Obstacles in halls/rooms?
- ** Area rugs are UNSAFE! They are a tripping hazard and hamper mobility for people using walkers or wheelchairs.
- Use of Facilities: Do residents have use of the kitchen? Activity rooms? Dining room? Grounds? Kitchens and utility rooms are dangerous for clients with dementia and confusion. Are these rooms easily accessible and/or secured for residents?
- Smoking Policy: Ask about their smoking policy, both for

residents and staff.

- Personal Furnishings: What furniture is provided? Can your loved one bring his or her own? Recliners are a favorite place for many seniors; is one available? Or, ask if your loved one can bring their own.
- Visiting hours: What are the visiting hours, if any, and do you have to call first?

Staff & Residents

- Are residents clean, well dressed, and well groomed?
- Are they slouching and sleeping in front of a television, or having fun watching an old Western?
- Are residents engaged in exercises or activities?

Accommodations

- Ask to see the different kinds of rooms: Shared Room, Private Bedroom with Private Bath, and Private Bedroom with Shared Bath

- Security

- Controlled access, especially a monitored exit is very important.
- Call buttons for residents is a nice plus. So are beds or chair alarms for residents who tend to get up without assistance and who are at risk of falls.

Amenities

- Air purification.
- Cable hook-up.
- Climate control.
- Private telephone line or cable – included? TV often is, but not phone line.
- Is there a walk-in shower?

Types of Personal Assistance

- Thoroughly discuss, and clearly understand what care can be provided, and what the care limitations are.

- Will the staff help with activities of daily living (bathing, grooming, dressing, eating, etc.)?
- Catheter management?
- Foot care?
- Assistance with sitting, standing, and walking?
- Toileting and incontinence care?
- Medication management. If diabetic, ask if injections can be given in the home.

Dementia Services

- Are family members invited to participate in the Care Plan? (That is the law!)
- Specialty trained staff must have Dementia Specialty and Mental Dementia or Mental Health Specialty should be noted on the AFH license.
- Are there safe wandering areas available?
- Does the facility undergo regular assessments by interdisciplinary staff?
- Is the environment easy to navigate?
- Are there difficult-behavior-reducing activities planned? Activities should be tailored to resident's needs.

Social and Personal Comfort and Desires

- Outings: Shopping, drives, religious services, etc. What costs are involved?
- In-home exercises or activities? What are they, and are they planned?
- Ask about what activity calendar in place right now.
- Hobbies: Can the home support or accommodate personal hobbies?
- Religion: Is there a religious preference in the home?
- Pets: Are they allowed to visit or can your loved one bring their own pet?

10 Hallmarks of a Great Adult Family Home

Obviously, every person has their own personal sense of style, quality, and what a "good home" means to them—it's a subjective issue. That said, a number of common traits are typically present in homes that most people consider high quality.

Some people say, "how you do one thing is how you do everything."

There are several pointers that will quickly give you a good indication if you are looking at a quality Adult Family Home, and I'm going to give the bottom line right here.

Often, the details and the small stuff you notice gives you a clue about the level of attention your loved one might receive in that home. So I encourage you to be as mindful as possible during your visit to any care facility.

1. **Attractive and well kept. When you go for a scheduled visit, the facility knows you are coming and should be putting their best foot forward. Make sure the facility is well taken care of without obvious signs of disrepair.**

2. **Odor free. When you first walk in, you should NOT note any obvious odors. But if there are smells, they should be fresh, light, and of food and baking. Strong air fresheners often mask persistent bad smells.**

3. **Residents are clean, well dressed, and well groomed. Even if residents are severely disabled, they should appear to be happy and well. Be aware that many seniors with dementia can and do suffer from anxiety and delusions, and as a person not used to being around such disability you may feel at odds… it's natural, but they should still "look good" in general.**

4. **The provider/owner and the staff have a happy demeanor and clear communication skills. Make sure you talk to the staffs that interact with residents on a day-to-day basis and not just the owner. Engage the staff by asking open-ended questions such as, "How long have you worked here?" and, "What do you like most about this adult family home?"**

5. The home is free of clutter, tripping hazards, and is well-lit. Problem areas include area rugs or too much furniture. There is good light, ideally natural lighting. The home should be clear and bright enough so as to emanate "a happy feeling," and you should have no trouble seeing well.

6. The house is clean! I know everyone has different standards of cleanliness, but if you look on the floor, it should be clean and dust-free. Look at light-switch plates – always a good indicator! Are the beds neatly made?

7. The floor plan is straightforward. Complicated twists and turns tend to confuse residents, even visitors!

8. The medication storage is clean and well organized. Look at the medication log paperwork, a resident chart, and at the medication storage cabinet and system. You don't need to know what this "should look like" but if it's clean and organized, you'll recognize that.

9. The staff engages the residents in some fashion. The residents are NOT lined up in a row mindlessly watching television. An old favorite TV show or planned blockbuster movie is different, if used as a planned activity.

10. **The food looks appetizing and nutritious.** Try to visit during a meal if possible to check out the food. Look on counters… do you notice fresh fruit on the countertops?

Now you've got your list of Adult Family Homes and you what to look for when you visit. Time to hit the road!

How Do You Know If You Found a "Good" Care Home?

Quality standards can vary greatly from care home to care home. Ultimately, the best care home or setting is one that meets your present needs, can easily adapt to meet potential future care needs (see chapter on determining future needs), offers a high degree of safety by understanding the medical and physical challenges your loved one faces, and is able to implement a consistent care plan.

Remember that a good part of touring is perception; so trust your gut and go with instinct. Ask yourself these questions that go above and beyond what meets the eye.

- Did you feel welcome?
- Does the home, owner, and staff "feel good" to you?
- Did they answer your questions openly, thoroughly and willingly?
- Are the other residents a good fit for your loved one? Are they "compatible?"
- Do you believe your loved one will enjoy a higher quality of life here?

Let's look at some of the underlying attributes of a care home that might make it a good fit for you.

Convenience
The home should be convenient for you to visit or stop by on a dime, meaning it's close to work or home, or in-between. If the elderly person has a spouse who will visit but doesn't drive, you might want to make sure that the facility is on a bus route.

Consistency
There is a lot to be said for consistency; if you know what to expect and are able to trust and rely upon a consistent service and quality of care, you'll have more peace of mind, even if it isn't the "royal treatment."

Cleanliness
Somebody wise said, "How we do one thing is how we do everything." How

clean and tidy a home is *does* reflect care and attention to detail. Cleanliness should meet *your* standards.

Safe Systems
Again, you're looking for systems that are already in place with other residents or in the home, including call bells, alarm sensors to alert staff when residents try to get up without calling for help, awake night staff, good record-keeping, etc.

Other safety concerns include rugs and area carpets, clutter, no handrails, not enough grab bars.
Good Communication with Provider AND Staff.

You'll be dealing with a care provider and his staff for a long time, so make sure there are no language and communication barriers.

7 Tips to Help you Gauge Trust and Consistency

Plan to visit at least twice after you've narrowed your options – three or four visits are even better.
Try arriving unannounced or on short notice, perhaps when other families are likely to visit.
Encourage comments about care while you observe and consider the following. Visit during a meal.

1. Does the provider/staff encourage you to talk freely, ask questions, and speak to other residents?
2. Are your observations consistent?
3. Are the other residents an appropriate match for your loved one?
4. Are residents treated with dignity and respect?
5. Do the staff and provider seem organized?
6. Do the staff and provider show respect by knocking on the resident's door before introducing you?
7. Ask for a list of references for their CURRENT residents (family members or advocates) and CALL THEM!

If you can answer YES to these questions and you feel the home can provide a good care environment, you've likely found a good match.

Be sure you have a completed copy of the <u>Basic Level Of Care Assessment</u>

and your personalized list of interview questions ready, bring a touring partner, and you're ready to rock these interviews!

The 6 Facts You Must Know Before Hiring a Placement Service or Referral Agency

The Seattle Times recently reported that,

> *"Increasingly, elder-placement companies are embracing a Web-based business model, in which placements are brokered over the telephone — and commissions collected — without any personal [physical] contact."*

Washington is the first state to clamp down on the unregulated, explosive growth of elder-care referral businesses that rake in profits, sometimes deceptively, by promising to help families find long-term care for the aged.

The objective of this chapter is help you understand how the senior care referral system works so that you can make decisions that will best serve your interests.

You should know that some of the very best care homes out there do not work with referral agents – or only work with a select few. What that means is if you decide to work with a referral agent, you could miss out on some of the very best options!

Here is what we're going to cover:

- What are Senior Referral Agents?
- How do Referral Agencies Work?
- Historical Perspective on Referral Agents
- What to Expect When Working With A Referral Agent
- The 5 Types of Referral Agents
- Benefits and Drawbacks of Working with Referral Agents
- Disclosures You Must Receive – or Ask For

What are Senior Referral Agents and Agencies?

> *Simply put, referral and placement agents are contracted by long-term care facilities to bring them your business.*

In general, referral agents/agencies provide you, the elder care consumers, with referrals to Adult Family Homes, Assisted Living Facilities, Nursing

Homes, and now even home care services. Senior Referral Agents can be individuals, nurses, former marketing directors, elder care providers, or Certified Senior Advisors (CSA).

Referral agents who are CSA's boast that fact. Certified Senior Advisors have a broad knowledge spectrum, which is convenient, but by and large still do not have a medical or nursing background. Many CSA's are often realtors, financial advisors, or social services professionals who want to cater to seniors, and being a CSA is the perfect addition to their main area of knowledge, but by no mean is it the end-all-be-all skill relative to placements and long-term care.

> *Most "bed brokers" have no experience providing nursing or personal care to seniors.*

Many senior care advisors do not personally know the care facility to which they are referring you. And most importantly, their referral list contains only care facilities they receive a referral fee from, leaving you with limited options.

> *Even though there may be a better financial or environmental fit for you elsewhere, referral agents only promote the facilities they have a monetary incentive to.*

How Do Referral Agencies Work?

Each referral service contracts with several facilities, typically based on their geographical area, and sometimes based on a facility's specialty. Some large online placement services such as A Place For Mom and Care Patrol have referral contracts nationwide and advisors located in most major metropolitan areas.

Once you select a facility that was shown by the agent, the agent will receive a referral fee from the facility or care provider based on the contract terms, typically 100% of your monthly care fee. Although there are still some agents charging a 50% referral fee, the majority charge 100%.
This is why their service is "free to you."

What to Expect When Working With A Referral Agent

The typical process goes like this: you are looking for an elder care facility in your area, you fill out an online form, and you are quickly contacted by a referral "advisor" who are likely working from home offices. While some "advisors" are professionally equipped to handle issues dealing with the elderly, the majority are not.

The advisor or placement agent will first ask you to commit to using them, but remember this:

> *Starting in 1013, a legally binding commitment is not allowed in Washington State so you can stop using a referral agent anytime and for any reason.*

Then, they'll proceed to interview you and ask questions about your current living situation, desired location, care needs of your loved one, personal preferences, and other relevant issues such as your budget – how much money you can afford to pay for care.

After this, they will schedule showings for you and perhaps escort you to visit 2 or 3 care homes or assisted living facilities.

If you don't like any of the facilities presented to you, the agent will likely do exactly what you would: get a list of other care providers in your desired area and start calling!

They'll quickly seek to establish new contracts so they can show you these additional facilities and get paid if a successful placement ensues.

If a facility is not interested in a contract with that agent, that facility will not be part of the choices offered to you as an option for care.

As a long-time care provider in my city, I consistently receive one to two calls a week from agents who are working with prospective customers who already know from their own research they are specifically interested in my care homes. Sadly, these clients are rarely shown my care homes when working with these agents due to the very high cost.

What happens if you've been looking on your own, then contact a referral agent?

If you've been looking at care homes on your own, then call a referral agent, it is nearly certain that you'll be discouraged from pursuing those options. In fact, I bet on it!

Be ready to hear a plethora of reasons in favor of stopping your own search, including:

- "We only work with the absolute best, and *that* home is not on our list."
- "I am not familiar with this provider, so I can't suggest it."
- "Let me help negotiate the transition and serve as an advocate for you."

If you really liked a home that you had previously seen, you may be coached to tell that care home owner that you are now working with the referral agent, and they will be representing you from now on.

Now you may ask, "but aren't they working to find me the best home? Aren't they advocating for my best interest?"

Yes, they *should*. But the simple reason is that if you work with any agent but pick a facility you found on your own, the agent would not receive a commission. It simply isn't worth their time to help you unless you pick a care home that's on their list.

Case in point. In the summer of 2010 a prospect of mine, Sarah, came to me on a personal reference from one of my previous clients. I was quite impressed with her due diligence. She came over for an initial tour, then twice more with siblings and her husband. Sarah called three of my references, and read our Residency Agreement and Policies – she came back with questions. I personally assessed her mother to ascertain her needs. Sarah was ready to move her 94-year old mother, "at your earliest convenience" she had told me.

Then Sarah got a call from a local referral agent, who I incidentally knew quite well, offering her to help with the transition. She advised Sarah to stop her proactive search, explaining that everything would be *much safer for her and her mom* if the agent was allowed, at no charge, to serve "as an advocate" during this transition.

Sarah soon discovered the agent's underlying motivation: a referral commission worth $5400. She immediately told the agent, "No thanks, I've already made my decision." Sadly, Sarah's mom passed away in late 2013, after 3-plus very happy years at Spada Homes.

An honest and ethical referral agent – yes, there are a few – will review what you've done so far, and encourage you to continue if you are on the right track. It promotes goodwill and takes just a few minutes. But the vast majority will try to convince you that you're on the wrong track and advise you to abandon those previous options and work with them instead.

Historical Perspective on Referral Agents

Beginning in the early 1990s, referral agents have been hired and commissioned by care providers, namely Adult Family Homes, to help increase occupancy rates. Even today, most Adult Family Home providers are poor advertisers and do not understand how to market their care homes and services. Because of this, referral agents have become an integral part of the marketing equation for the vast majority of care home owners and providers who don't have the inclination, time, or facility to develop relationships with other referral sources.

As more providers relied on the agencies and competition increased, so did commissions and financial incentives. Today, a standard commission is 100% of your first monthly care fee within just a few years.

As you can imagine, this kind of "fast and easy income" attracted a large number of new referral agents and the industry became over-saturated by people lured by the promise of high income and little work.

Why do I say "easy" income"? Because in many instances a single referral *call*, say 20-to-30 minutes on the phone, can result in a placement generating a sizeable commission check.

> *The market was ripe for the picking, with a super-easy sell to consumers – who doesn't want a "free senior placement service?"*

In Washington (and probably most other states), this industry was completely unregulated until 2012. After numerous complaints from providers and consumers, Lawmakers implemented legislation to start regulating the referral industry. However, those new regulations do not address or solve what is, in my humble opinion, a key issue: their *dual-agency nature*.

Meaning they represent you as the end-consumer and the care provider who pays for their service. And *the more you pay for care, the higher the commission checks.*

It is nearly impossible for a bed broker to advocate for your best interest when such large commissions are at stake.

BIG SECRETS No Placement Agent Wants You To Know

I want to caution you about referral agents who claim they have "pre-screened the facilities and providers on their list," and websites that say they "only bring you to the "best" care homes and facilities".

What they are *likely* saying is they may have checked the facility's citation history, and possibly made in-person visits.

Monitoring each care community for safety, quality, complaint history, and violations is not only incredibly difficult, it's a losing financial proposition for any referral agency. To begin, many safety and care issues are hard to detect, for example skin integrity problems such as bedsores; these problems require physical examination by a competent, educated, and licensed person. It simply takes way too much time, manpower and paperwork to track safe care in facilities, even doing so on an annual or quarterly basis. It's a nice idea, but unrealistic and definitely not the norm.

A more recent and growing practice is for quality professional placement services to check the Department of Social and Health Services (DSHS) for what is called an "Enforcement Letter." Enforcement letters are issued to providers who have unresolved or repeated violations. It takes less than five minutes to do this, and anyone can do it since it is in the public records system. To see if compliance records are available in your State, you'll need to check with your State's Department of Health office or website.

> *You must keep in mind that 99% of the agents visit care facilities like you do: on a scheduled basis. As on your first visit, they accompany you on scheduled showings and rarely, if ever, take time to visit homes on a regular or consistent basis, let alone do thorough inspections or un-scheduled visits to spot problems. It is common practice for a new referral agent to come tour the care home just before they bring you along for the first visit.*

Case in point. The Federal Trade Commission (FTC) recently charged two referral agencies, CarePatrol and ABCSP (dba Always Best Care Senior Services) with misleading consumers by claiming that they had done extensive research on care facilities and offered recommendations on their alleged legwork.

Rather than fight the case – or do more in-depth research – CarePatrol and ABCSP agreed to settle with the FTC and were forced to revise their marketing messages.

Common Myths about Why Referral Services are "FREE" to You

"Our services are *always free* to seniors and their families. There is *never* a cost to you." When you ask how such valuable services can be "free," a prevalent statement you will hear is: "*We are funded by the housing industry.*" The statement is not technically false, but it misleads you to believe that there is wide-spread support for the service and that there is some sort of industry funded program to pay for this free service – there is definitely *not*.

> *Reality check: there is NO such industry funding – there are only individual providers and facilities that agree, under contract, to pay referral fees to acquire your business! And that's why it's free to you.*

Nearly all referral agencies charge the selected provider a fee for your referral. As mentioned earlier, most agencies charge between 50% and 100% of the monthly care fee you pay the provider, with the majority trending toward 100%.

Regardless of the percentage, these fees add up to thousands of dollars per placement.
Here is some quick math for perspective; if a care facility charges $5,000 per month for care, that provider will pay a referral fee as follows:

1. 100% = $5,000 referral fee (majority of agents)
2. 75% = $3,750 referral fee (few)
3. **50% = $2,500 referral fee (rare)**

Another BIG secret – whenever you move, they get richer.
If you become unhappy in your chosen care facility, the referral agent will get

richer. I know that sounds harsh but unfortunately the following is a widespread practice.

Say after 2 or 3 months you decide the care facility isn't a good fit. You call your referral agent back and she helps you explore another option. You decide to move ahead with the new choice. When your loved one is moved, the new care provider *will pay a full referral fee.*

Very few placement contracts include refund or grace period clauses so essentially your business can mean two—or more—referral fees collected.

The 5 Types of Referral Agents

1. **Internet-Based Referral Websites**

   - Large companies, some multi-state. Many of the advisors do not know homes or providers personally and build relationships by phone. (Described above.)
   - They are largely Internet-based and technology companies that rely on the vast reach of the World Wide Web to attract as many potential leads as possible. They are primarily interested in building a large database of potential clients. Then follow up with you by phone, give you a list, and collect the placement fee.

2. **Medium-Size Senior Care and Housing Options Agencies**

   - Some referral and placement agencies have 3 to 10 placement advisors. As above, they only refer to contracted facilities. If they are local, chances are higher that they know the care providers personally – and that's a good thing because they are more likely to get feedback from clients as to the quality of care provided in that care facility.
   - Since they are usually local, it allows them to establish trust and note the provider's consistency.

3. **Nurses**

   - Registered nurses often drive the smaller placement agencies. If you're going to work with a referral agent, they are a good option. Nurses have a keen eye for good care and a strong background in direct care.

- Nurses usually know a handful of providers and often establish stronger and long-lasting relationships with those providers. They get to know and trust them. Even though they also limit their referrals to contracted providers, the quality of the options presented to you is likely to be high. After all, their personal reputation is on the line.
- Nurses can help ensure the care plan is adequate, and they know first-hand if that provider has actually demonstrated their ability to care for certain difficult residents.

4.   Adult Family Home Providers

- These are care home providers who decided to become part-time placement agents. Their primary purpose is to fill their own beds. The overflow often goes to family members who own other care homes, and lastly, to other providers.
- These providers also charge fees for their referrals. The most important thing to remember is that you want FULL DISCLOSURE so that you fully understand the arrangements, and how a potential conflict of interest may impact you.

5.   Geriatric Care Manager

- Geriatric care managers are technically NOT considered referral agents/agencies because *they are not compensated for referrals*. It goes against a Geriatric Care Manager's ethical model to contract for referral fees. And that makes them an ideal choice because there is no conflict of interest present – you pay for services rendered, i.e. time. They are free to act in your best interest and again, have no financial incentives based on how much you pay for care, or where you go.
- Unfortunately, because there is little financial reward for them, they often defer the placement portion of their job to a referral agent… so you may be back to square one!

Benefits and Drawbacks of Working with a Referral Agent

I don't endorse nor condemn working with referral agents. In fact, I have enjoyed very fruitful long-term working relationships with several nurses' referral agents in the Puget Sound region over the years.

But there are pros and cons of working with referral agents, and my job is to cut through the noise and tell you what you most need to know in order to make an informed decision.

Benefits

1.   **Speed**. In general, using a referral agent can shorten the time it takes to find a good care home, because referral agents are more familiar with the local options. This is especially valuable when you need a placement fast, due to emergency circumstances.

2.   **Support.** Working with a referral agent can give you a sense of support and someone to discuss your questions or concerns with.

Drawbacks

1.   **No Medicaid Placements.** If you receive Medicaid or other Federal funding for your care, referral agents will not help you. By law, they are not allowed to collect placement fees or other compensation for helping a Medicaid recipient. If this is your case, you can hire a Geriatric Care Manager or get a list from the DSHS Aging and Disability Administration's <u>office website</u>.

2.   **Partial Menu.** Referral agents show care facilities with which they have a "placement contract" ensuring that their fees will be paid since they do not charge consumers (you) for services rendered. This means you won't see every care option, but only those pay your agent.

3.   **Geography.** Referral agents work within a defined geographical region, and with a limited number of care providers. This is both good and not so good. The good part is that they trust and like the providers they work with, and the bad is that your options are limited. If you don't like the options they present, they may search for additional care homes to show you; but unfortunately those care facilities will be new to the agent as well. And the first question they will ask that provider is, "Are you interested in setting up a referral contract?" Only then will they inquire about openings and care capability.

4.   **Best Match for... Who?** "We match you with the best care setting for your needs," is the most common marketing message from placement and referral agencies. Even though there may be a better financial or

environmental fit for you elsewhere, the referral agent promotes only facilities under contract. It is a very rare case for a referral agent to refer you to another agent who may be familiar with other facilities.

5. **Free in Front-End.** High referral fees ultimately drive care costs up. In the end, care providers must account for the cost of these high placement fees by raising their rates over the long run. Paying a 100% referral fee means a care provider will essentially have to give care at no charge for an entire month, incurring related costs such as staffing, etc.

Disclosures you MUST Receive in Washington State

When working with a referral agent or agency in Washington State, you must —by law—receive clearly spelled out disclosures, including:

- Commissions & referral fees paid to the agency, and by whom.
- Descriptions of services provided by the agency.
- Affiliations with, or ownership of care homes (or other facility or services to which they are referring you).
- Your consumer rights, and your right to discontinue using the agent/agency at any time, with or without cause.
- Dual-agency statement, meaning that the agency represents both you as the consumer, and the paying party for referral services in the same transaction.
- Disclosure of your confidential health care information.
- Explanation of refund policies.
- Insurance and liability coverage (agency must have liability insurance).
- How to file a complaint regarding referral services.

Unfortunately, most senior care consumers I speak with never receive the disclosures, or they are referred to look for them online, something consumers rarely do. If you don't receive the disclosures as required, you might consider another referral service.

I firmly believe that empowering both you as the consumer and the Adult Family Home owner through education is the best way to improve the long-term care system without the burden of unnecessary expenses or regulatory glut.

It's my belief that the current long-term care referral system has a useful function, but the financial model upon which it is based is not in the consumer's best interest. To learn more about this topic, visit www.AdultFamilyHomesCentral.com.

5 Questions and Tips To Safeguard Your Interest

1. Do you own any of the care homes you refer me too?
2. Can you send me a copy of your fees and commissions?
3. When presented with potential care providers, ask, "Have you referred clients these homes in the past, and how well do you know those providers?"
4. What happens if I find a home on my own?
5. If I don't select a home from your list, how does it impact our working relationship?

Conclusion

So there you have it – probably more information than you ever wanted to know about elder care placements!

If you complete the <u>Easy Senior Care Assessment</u> provided and add your knowledge of your loved one's personality, you should have a clear vision of the type of home that will be the best fit. Armed with this knowledge, your search for a placement has a great chance of success so that your loved one will be able to "age in place".

About Assisted Living Facilities

Given the number of options for senior housing and care, how do you know which setting is right for you or your loved one? So far we've addressed Adult Family Homes in depth; let me touch on Assisted Living and Nursing Home facilities.

It isn't within the scope of this book to explain each of these settings in great detail, but we'll cover important differences so you know what to look for and can avoid being blind-sided.

Assisted Living Facilities (ALFs) are technically *boarding homes* that provide varying levels of board and care. Within this general category there are several sub-categories relative to the amount of care that each facility is licensed for and thereby required to provide.

The sub-categories of licensing in Washington state are:
- Assisted Living (AL)
- Adult Residential Care (ARC)
- Enhanced Adult Residential Care (EARC)
- Expanded Community Services (ECS)
- Dementia Care (DC)

Boarding homes assume responsibility for the safety and wellbeing of their residents. Services may include housing, meals, laundry, supervision, and varying levels of assistance with care. Some offer nursing care and even provide specialized care for people with mental health issues, developmental disabilities, or dementia (a.k.a. memory care).

Living arrangements vary from studio, to single or double rooms, to suites or apartments, and are usually within a multi-unit residential setting. Occupancy varies from seven to several hundred. Because the level of care they are licensed to provide varies so widely, it's critical to understand what to look for and what to ask.

Retirement and independent living *do not assume any responsibility* for the safety or wellbeing of the seniors who live in them, even though visiting nurses or home health aides often provide medical or personal care. That responsibility is on your shoulders and it's critical you understand that.

Pricing structure

Most assisted living facilities charge a basic monthly rent fee ranging from $1800 to $4500 (2013 estimates) that generally includes meals and housekeeping. All personal care assistance is billed "a la carte," meaning that for EACH AREA of need (i.e. bathing, medication management, dressing, incontinence care, etc.) there will be a separate fee tacked on to the monthly room and board charge.
In some of the more upscale facilities, residents routinely pay $4800 to $10,000 per month once services for their personal care are included.

Drawbacks

- In every case, the senior will be alone behind closed doors whenever they are in their quarters, which is one of the biggest safety risks. The only way to address this risk and reduce the potential for injuries and accidents is to hire caregivers to be with him or her inside the apartment. Regardless of who provides the supervision for care, the financial burden will be yours to bear.

- It is CRITICAL to understand that care services such as medication assistance, bathing, and other care are "scheduled," which means a staff member will come help with those tasks only when scheduled. Your loved one should be physically agile and mentally alert enough to care for themselves safely during periods of time between scheduled visits.

    9. Some assisted living facilities do offer on-call help that is accessible IF the senior is able to call for help!

Aging in Place and the Care Continuum in Assisted Living Facilities

In nine-out-of-ten cases, assisted living is a TEMPORARY home. Three quarters of all referral calls we receive are from folks residing in assisted living facilities who have been asked to move out, or who sadly sustained injury as a result of insufficient care.

Of course, most people would prefer not to move when their care needs increase, and because some assisted living homes can and do offer personal care assistance for changing needs, many are led to believe that they'll never move again – an idea that is only partially true.

The assisted living industry, having access to massive financial resources, has answered this demand by building hybrid facilities that combine assisted living with nursing care and Alzheimer's care units. Dual levels of care in the same community can accommodate an individual's declining health needs or that of a spouse to help minimize the need for relocating.

But I want you to keep in mind that even in facilities offering a continuum of care, chances are high you'll need to move to another wing, floor, unit, or room, ultimately experiencing a change in staff, residents, and surroundings. Consider it a "mini-relocation."

When is an Assisted Living Facility a Good Option?

Assisted Living Facilities can be ideal for the healthier, more active and social senior who no longer wishes to remain home alone and only needs minimal "support care" such as meals, housekeeping, and other minimal assistance.

When considering an assisted living facility, ask yourself...

- Can my loved one manage on her own *most of the time*, with only occasional scheduled assistance?
- Does she need only a small amount of attention? Are her medical issues fairly straightforward and stable?
- Is she unlikely to fall? (If there is a history of falling, reconsider.)
- Are her mental faculties intact?
- Does she like being around many other people and take advantage of social opportunities?

If the answer to these questions is "Yes," an assisted living facility may be a very good fit.

Again, be prepared to transition to another facility as your loved one's condition or needs change.
These transitions become more difficult and stressful as people age or experience cognitive decline.

About Nursing Homes

Nursing Home placements are typically need-driven more than choice-driven. Generally, individuals end up in Nursing Homes because of an event that sends them to a hospital from their own home, a retirement home, or an assisted living facility.

These events often involve a fall resulting in broken bones (often the hips), surgery, stroke, cardiac episodes, or significant illness. On other occasions a socially and physically isolated senior becomes ill due to malnutrition, dehydration, or failure to follow their medication regimen.

As urgent medical needs are handled and the senior is deemed medically stable, the hospital's discharge planning frequently involves a nursing home stay. Nursing Homes differ from other care settings because they offer a full complement of medical professionals on staff, including Social Workers, Dieticians, Physical and Occupational Therapists, and 24-hours per day skilled nursing.

In either case, if the person needs skilled nursing care or rehabilitation services by a team of professional therapists, a Nursing Home is generally the proper setting.

When is a Nursing Home the Best Option?

Some people not only require extensive physical assistance, but they may also have chronic or acute medical conditions such as difficulty swallowing, violent behaviors requiring restraints, or morbid obesity. These are all conditions for which a nursing home is likely the best option.

As an alternative, some Adult Family Homes are owned and operated by skilled medical professionals and may offer specialized services that make them an attractive option even when a resident is experiencing difficult medical circumstances.

For example, one of my own residents moved out of a nursing home to come live with us despite extensive and complicated medical issues; chronic knee replacement hardware infections involving a wound that needs regular dressing changes, in addition to being overweight, wheelchair-bound, and suffering from other medical issues.

He has regained more mobility, enjoying closer and more meaningful relationships. A team of medical professionals monitors his status and progress, and according to his family, he's actually thriving for the first time in years.

Payment of Nursing Home Costs

Medicare part A typically covers a period of 30 to 90 days of nursing home costs directly following a hospital stay. After that period has passed, a patient is usually discharged to another long-term care (LTC) setting such as an Adult Family Home.

Those who wish to remain in the Nursing Home by choice—a rare occurrence—must pay privately or qualify for Medicaid assistance. Long-term care insurance policies often cover Nursing Home care.

The cost for a private-pay nursing home bed varies from region to region, but as a national average you can expect to pay as follow:

- Average price for a private room: $239 per night (up to $365 in Seattle)
- Median price for a shared room: $222 per night

Financially Driven Nursing Home Placements. Individuals who require state assistance for long-term care (Medicaid) have fewer and fewer choices relative to the provision of long-term care and housing. Because of this, Nursing Homes often become a principal alternative.

Monitoring Care in Long-Term Care Facilities

How do you know if your loved one is getting quality care? What do you look for, how do you spot problems, and if you have a suspicion of problems, what do you do?

Understandably, most of us are worried about placing our loved one in a care facility, especially if they are frail and vulnerable. We worry about abuse, neglect, and other undesirable issues the media tends to churn out as front-page news.

When is the last time you heard anything positive about long-term care?

We'd like to feel that someone has this issue under control, perhaps the state licensing authority or Ombudsman program. Failing those, there are also plenty of referral agencies and other resident advocates out there supposedly monitoring and keeping watch.

Recently, the referral agency CarePatrol was cited by the Federal Trade Commission (FTC) for falsely claiming they were monitoring facilities' licensing and citation history. To be candid, third party facility monitoring is not a reality or even a realistic probability.

> *Only two parties have enough "skin in the game," to manage this job: you, or someone you pay to do it, such as a geriatric care manager. It's not likely anyone else will invest the time, effort, or money this responsibility requires.*

No matter where your loved one resides, it's important that YOU understand how to monitor their safety and the quality of care they are receiving.

> *The best way to ensure safety in any long-term care facility is to stay personally involved. If you can't be, hire and pay a professional to do so in your stead.*

Care Plan: Make sure you understand and agree to a clear care plan. This plan should address the various aspects of the resident's needs such as physical, emotional, behavioral, social, and safety needs. Obtain a copy and review it periodically with the manager or administrator. If your loved is cognitively able to participate, involve them as well.

Routine Care Conferences: I suggest that you actually sit down with the manager or administrator and go over the care plan together every 90 days or so, and every time there is significant change in health status. This can easily be done in 30-45 minutes.

Talk With the Staff: Direct care staff can provide valuable specifics about your loved one's happenings and needs. Never feel shy about asking them clear and specific questions about care needs.

Concerns: Do you have concerns? In every case, your first step should be to discuss them immediately with the administrator or owner of the facility. Make a clear plan to identify and address every issue that is of concern to you and schedule a follow-up on the spot.

7 Signs of Poor Care or Possible Abuse

In this section you will learn how to determine signs of poor care or possible abuse.

The first thing you should do in the event you notice any issue described below is to try and determine the exact cause of the problem. Then you should find out what, if any, preventative measures were in place, and if so, were they followed?

Answering those two critical questions should make your next action step clear.

1.   **General Care**. Whenever you visit, be observant of the staff. Are they actually following the plan of care during their interactions with the resident?

   a.   If in a nursing home or assisted living facility, ask nursing aides who are providing care if they have seen the care plan and if it is reviewed with them regularly or when changes are made.

   b.   Is your loved one well-groomed and wearing clean clothing?

2.   **Trouble Eating**. Visit at mealtimes to monitor food quality and intake.

   a.   Are they getting necessary assistance from staff? It may seem basic, but when a resident can't cut meat with a knife and fork or open a yogurt container, for example, they simply won't eat it. Food left on the plate does nothing to nourish the body.

3.   **Weight Loss**. Residents should have their weight monitored by scale monthly and the results reviewed noting trends or changes. If there is a cardiac diagnosis and/or they are on diuretic medication, they should be weighed more frequently. You can also visually watch for signs of weight loss by inspecting upper arms and calves. Excessive sagging skin may be a sign of weight loss.

4.   **Dehydration**. Check hydration status by using this trick: gently grab and pinch some forearm skin between your thumb and index finger (grab superficial skin only, not flesh or muscle). The skin will bunch between your fingers to form a tent-shaped lump, but should quickly

disappear when you let go. The longer it takes for the skin to return to its original position, the more dehydrated they are. Dry lips and constipation are other signs of dehydration. Ask the staff to make sure water is accessible to the resident.

5.   **Pressure Ulcers**. For good reasons, "bed sores" invoke thoughts of abuse and neglect. Pressure ulcers are known as *bedsores* and *decubitus ulcers*.

   a.   Residents at risk for pressure ulcers are those who have poor mobility, low weight, malnutrition, dehydration, incontinence, sedation, poor circulation, and end-of-life transitions. You should know that although it's not always easy, pressure ulcers are *generally* preventable. While prevention strategies are achievable in every setting, the inevitable physical decline of most residents, especially those near the end of life, sometimes make preventing pressure ulcers difficult.

   b.   If your loved one is at risk, that risk should be identified and addressed in the care plan.

   c.   Pressure ulcer prevention relies on managing risk factors. It's imperative to use best-practices to manage diminished mobility, pressure to bony areas that compromise blood flow to areas of potential breakdown, shearing and friction that occur due to prolonged immobility, poor nutritional status, and prolonged skin contact with moisture.

   d.   Check to see if the staff is following preventive measures such as proper cushioning (using egg crate or air mattress on beds and chairs) for high-risk areas such as heel, elbows, shoulders, and hips. These residents should be repositioned frequently – usually every hour or two.

   e.   Visually check for developing pressure sores and other signs of skin breakdown. Inspect heels, elbows, sacral, or coccyx area (tailbone), upper back, ear cartilage, and any bony areas like the shoulder blades.

   f.   If you see redness, press directly on it. It will immediately whiten (that's called blanching). If the redness returns as you remove pressure, it means that tissue integrity is already compromised and the resident is at high risk for worsening skin breakdown. This stage requires action to prevent further problems and is categorized as a "Stage I" pressure sore.

g.   Ask staff to help with this task so you can evaluate and discuss any finding immediately. If you can make this a routine, you'll manage this inside of 5 minutes.

6.   **Offensive Smells**. This is a frequent problem with incontinent residents, but when the staff is attentive and prompt, offensive odors should be infrequent. If you notice offensive smells every time you visit, it should raise your concern.

a.   Note whether staff are available to assist the resident to the bathroom when needed or on a regular schedule if necessary.

b.   If adult incontinent briefs are used, determine whether usage is based on need or convenience. You can know how often they are being changed by monitoring how many diapers are being used in a 24-hour period. Do keep in mind, however, that sometimes an incontinent resident may need less frequent diaper changes if they are being assisted to the bathroom on a regular schedule, no matter whether they are soiled or not.

c.   Reddened, irritated, or excoriated skin on the buttocks is a sign of poor hygiene and mismanaged incontinence care.

7.   **Bruising & Injuries**. First, you need to understand the difference between a bruise, and other "bruise-like" conditions such as senile purpura. "Deep tissue" bleeding causes a bruise. Key findings include induration (hardening) over the area, and changing colors going from blue/black to purple, then green, then yellow. The discoloration eventually disappears altogether. On the other hand, *senile purpura* is caused by superficial bleeding of the capillaries and produces a fairly bright purple coloring. There is rarely hardening and the color remains fairly constant and can remain for several months, sometimes permanently. Also, keep in mind:

a.   Medications that cause bruising include aspirin, Coumadin (a blood thinner), anti-inflammatory such as Advil, and corticosteroids.

b.   Bruising that should cause concern are those located near genitals or breasts, wrists or ankles, face and neck, buttocks, bottom of feet, or abdomen.

c.   Recurring or frequent bruising may not be accidental.

d.   Accidental bruising may include areas involved in transferring residents, such as arms, armpits, or forearms.

Stay alert, visit often, and as I mentioned earlier, the best way to ensure the safety of a loved one in any long-term care facility is to stay personally involved – there really is no way around this one.

State-Issued Enforcement Letters – The Basics

Enforcement letters are more serious than citations. Most, if not all, care homes and long-term care facilities end up with deficiencies and citations at some point if they are around for any length of time – it's almost unavoidable, but not necessarily a sign of trouble.

For example, if a staff of 5 years was late in renewing her yearly food handler's permit once, it doesn't mean she's become incompetent, but as far as state licensing is concerned, that staff has now "placed residents at risk of acquiring food-borne illnesses," (or a similar declaration) and the facility gets a citation. The citation will never mention details, perhaps "caregiver was registered to renew her permit within 8 days of expiration," but only that "provider failed to ensure compliance with the law, placing residents at risk of food poisoning."

Enforcement letters, on the other hand are a more serious issue—usually. I say *usually* because in the last few years many enforcement letters are issued simply because of a late or unpaid licensing fee.
Event with an enforcement letter, no resident harm may have occurred (in many cases), but it's a sign that a care provider is either unable to manage the State rules and regulations, repeatedly cited for the same issues, or possibly unable to provide safe care due to a "deficient practice."

Some enforcement letters can be issued after a single violation if the licensor believes the problem exposes residents to increased risk of harm. Sometimes an enforcement letter includes a *stop placement*, meaning a care provider cannot admit new residents until such restrictions are lifted.

Rules and regulations governing long-term care facilities in Washington are not only very extensive, but much of them are written in broad terms, allowing for rather liberal interpretations by licensing staff and care providers. Here is an example:

> *"The adult family home must promote care for residents in a manner and in an environment that maintains or enhances each resident's dignity and respect in full recognition of his or her individuality."*

So ideally I suggest that you pick a facility without any recent enforcement letters, and if an enforcement letter was issued in the past, make certain you understand what it was for so you can monitor any concerns closely.

Enforcement letters remain on the provider's public record, even after they have been rescinded by the state.

If you are really interested in a certain provider and they have an enforcement letter, you should definitely examine the enforcement letter AND recent inspection reports to determine why the letter was issued. Was it a simple matter such as a late licensing fee renewal payment, or more serious safety concerns?

It may require keen judgment to separate what is truly relevant from what isn't. I strongly suggest that you get help from a professional.

How to Check for an Enforcement Letter in 5 Minutes or Less

A good time to determine if an enforcement letter has been issued is *before* your very first visit to a care home or facility. Contrary to popular belief, this is quick and easy to do. You don't need any special access, skill, or knowledge – just a computer with Internet access, and the following instructions.

Here is how to check:

- Go to the appropriate DSHS website page for

    a) <u>Adult family homes</u>
    b) <u>Boarding Homes / Assisted living</u>
    c) <u>Nursing Homes</u>

- **Search Criteria**: select the County, City, or ZIP code to locate the facility in question
- **Specific Criteria**: in the "Enforcement Letters" selection box, choose and click on "Show Only Facilities WITH Enforcement Letters"

    a) On the results page, look for the facility in question. Hopefully your desired facility *is not listed* on this page!
    b) Conversely, you can select "show all facilities" and locate the specific home in question, then see if there is an enforcement letter.

You can also watch a <u>video tutorial here</u>.

Appendix 1

Medical Industry Certifications and License Types Demystified

Ever wonder what those abbreviations after names mean? There are so many and to most people, they can all sound so similar! Here is a brief explanation of those that you are most likely to encounter as you research Adult Family Homes or other long-term care facilities.

Let's start with those abbreviations, their actual title and a short description of education and/or general qualifications as they pertain to a senior's day-to-day care:

MD   Medical Doctor
There are very few Medical Doctors in the Adult Family Home industry. If you encounter one, make sure you understand WHY they are in the business.

DNP   Doctor of Nursing Practice
Just a few in Washington State. Advanced nursing degree with a Masters, then a doctorate or PhD in nursing practice. DNPs often practice as primary care providers.

ARNP   Advanced Registered Nurse Practitioner
Usually has prescriptive authority and works under the supervision of a Medical Doctor. But on a day-to-day basis, they assume primary responsibility for the management of medical care.

RN   Registered Nurse (See Table Below)
LPN   Licensed Practical Nurse (See Table Below)

NA-C (CNA)   Nursing Assistant Certified
Requires about 40 to 50 hours of class time, plus 40 to 60 hours of supervised clinical practice in a skilled nursing facility. Standardized Testing to certify is required.

NA-R (RNA)   Nursing Assistant Registered
No educational requirements except AIDS and HIV training, plus an application fee (about $30 in Washington) to the Department of Health are the only requirements to receive a NA Registration.

CGCP   Certified Geriatric Care Provider

Program specifically designed for Adult Family Home providers. This program is offered through the University Of Washington School Of Nursing, and requires a minimum of 75 hours of specialized lectures followed by testing. DSHS issues a "Notice of Geriatric Certification."

PT   Physical Therapist

Physical Therapists are trained to identify and maximize quality of life and movement potential within the spheres of promotion, prevention, diagnosis, treatment/intervention, and rehabilitation.

OT   Occupational Therapist

Occupational Therapists are trained to modify the physical environment as well as training to use assistive equipment to increase independence. Their focus is to help their patients engage in meaningful activities of daily living (ADLs).

CSA   Certified Senior Advisor

Up to 35 hours of training applies to general knowledge of health, social, and financial issues and how these factors work together in seniors' lives.

MA   Medical Assistant

General skills such as vital signs assessments, blood draws, EKGs, and similar medical office tasks. Curriculum doesn't include training to provide personal care.

What's the Difference Between an NA-R and NA-C?

A **Nursing Assistant-Registered** must complete the NA Registration Form and pay an annual fee to the Department of Health. No personal care training or educational requirements are needed, aside from AIDS/HIV training. The Department of Health (DOH) keeps NA names on a registry.

A **Nursing Assistant-Certified** has completed an educational program (see above), passed a standardized state test, and has been awarded the credential of NA-C (formerly CNA). They also pay a fee, renew annually, and are listed on the DOH registry. Both NA-Rs and NA-Cs may be disciplined under the Uniform Disciplinary Act.

Registered Nurse (RN) vs. Licensed Practical Nurse (LPN) – What

is The Difference?

This is not meant to be an exhaustive or exact explanation of every difference, but I want to outline the main differences, especially as they relate to day-to-day nursing care as provided in geriatric care settings such as Adult Family Homes.

First and foremost, both are licensed under the same WAC (Washington Administrative Code) and both are accountable for their independent judgment through the Uniform Disciplinary Act.

Registered Nurses are normally in charge of care planning, complex nursing procedures, and are often in managerial positions. **Licensed Practical Nurses** focus on practical skills to provide direct patient care. In recent years, many care facilities and medical institutions hire LPNs in quantities due to the fact that they are more affordable and once trained for the job, LPNs will deliver skilled care for a fraction of the cost.

Registered Nurses' educational backgrounds are much broader. For a basic 2-year RN degree, a full year is dedicated to general education and sciences, as compared to LPN, where their one-year degree is focused on practical skills.

Any nurse—RN or LPN—can, and often must acquire specialized training in order to provide specialized care. Examples of specialized care include geriatric care, surgery, or cardiac care. Career-wise, RNs hold positions such as Director of Nursing, or administrators, but LPNs rarely, if ever, do.

About RN and LPN Education?

RN: A 2-year, full-time college degree process. A Bachelor's degree can be earned with 4 years (BSN – Bachelor's in Nursing).

LPN: A 1-year full-time, or 2-year part-time college degree process.

Education Differences

RN: General education prerequisites plus more sciences as part of the curriculum.

LPN: General sciences as prerequisites.

Advanced Nursing

- Bachelors and Masters in Nursing for RNs
- Advanced Registered Nurse Practitioner (ARNP)
- Doctor of Nursing Practice (DNP)
- No advanced practice available to LPNs; only specialized post-education training and/or certifications.

Accountability

- Both RNs and LPNs use independent nursing judgment, and both are accountable for their own actions under the Department of Health Uniform Disciplinary Act.

Licensing

- An **RN** is licensed after passing the national exam (NCLEX-RN).
- An **LPN** is licensed after passing the national exam (NCLEX-PN).

Real-Life Practice

- **RNs** tend to design the care plan, and LPNs implement it (especially in nursing home & hospital settings).
- **Like RNs, LPNs** can give shots, change wound dressings, clean and bandage wounds, administer medications, give injections, monitor patient condition, assess vital signs, and are trained to do care planning and monitor patient conditions and progress. In Adult Family Homes, Assisted Living, and some Nursing Homes, LPNs are very involved in care planning and oversee the Nursing Assistant's implementation of care plans.

Appendix 2

Understanding Hospice Care

The purpose of Hospice is to meet the emotional, spiritual, and physical needs of people dealing with a terminal illness and end-of-life care.

Hospice focuses on pain and symptom management rather than trying to cure or control a disease. That being said, some treatments such as antibiotics may be used to increase comfort if appropriate, but typically are not used with the intention of extending or prolonging life.

Who is eligible?

Hospice care is a federal program that is also funded by the state, and is provided to persons facing the advancing stages of a terminal illness with no hopes of remission.

Where is care provided?

Hospice care is provided in the privacy and comfort of the patient's home or other places of residence such as Adult Family Homes, skilled nursing facilities, and some assisted living facilities.

Who pays for Hospice?

Hospice care is covered by most insurers, including Medicare, Medicaid, and many private insurance policies. Some Hospice agencies admit qualifying patients regardless of their ability to pay.

For more information regarding Hospice, go to http://www.wshpco.org/ or talk with your loved one's physician.

What if my loved one lives at home? Is remaining at home through the end of life an option?

Yes. While remaining at home for the elderly can be a costly option even in the best of times, mainly due to staffing costs, they can remain in their home through end of life if finances are not a concern.

You should know that Hospice staff generally only provides 24-hour care, called Continuous Home Care, during "brief periods" of crisis. Even if qualified, this may consist only of 8-hour per day continuous, or in two 4-hour shifts, and will only remain in force during times of acute need.

This means that for long-term, day-to-day care needs, Hospice care will not be a feasible option.
In general, you can expect Hospice to provide the primary instruction for delivering your loved one comfortable care, but only limited staff on a day-to-day basis.

Benefits:

- Most people would prefer to remain in the environment they know and love.
- More potential for comfort, privacy, and space for family, friends, and caregivers.
- More freedom of choice in end-of-life setting, such as spaciousness in surroundings, music, art, etc.

Drawbacks:

- High cost – especially if your loved one needs care on a 24-hour basis.
- The physical, emotional, and/or financial costs can be substantial. This is usually true when remaining at home, whether or not they are in end-of-life stage.
- It is the family's responsibility to find, train, supervise, and monitor any staff.
- Skill level and training requirements of Home Aid caregivers is lower than that of Adult Family Home providers or other licensed settings.
- When hiring private care from the newspaper or Craigslist, you may find potential caregivers who appear knowledgeable, but do not have the necessary training and qualifications to provide safe care.
- Strangers are constantly in your home.
- Social isolation and sensory deprivation is very common, often driving people into Adult Family Homes.

10.

Regardless of what setting you are considering for yourself or your loved one, be sure to ask if Hospice care is possible while touring facilities.

Appendix 3

Is Elder Care Tax Deductible?

I've spoken with our tax accountant to better understand the various tax rules relative to tax-deductible expense for long-term care costs. **The following information is not to be considered legal or tax advice.** Tax laws change frequently, and you should consult with a CPA before making important decisions about your tax liability or income tax returns.

That being said, I have good news for you: in most cases "qualified" long-term care expenses are tax-deductible.

Qualified long-term care services you receive are deductible from your gross income as an itemized deduction to the extent that your (the taxpayer's) total of unreimbursed medical expenses exceeds 7.5% of your adjusted gross income.

Okay, what does that mean? If you pay for your long-term care out of pocket AND you're not being reimbursed by insurance (for example), AND that cost is more than 7.5% of your adjusted gross income, you can deduct the expense.

Earlier, I used the phrase "qualified" long-term care services. That means necessary diagnostic, preventive, therapeutic, curing, treating, mitigating, and rehabilitative services and **maintenance or personal care services** that are *required* by a chronically ill individual and that are *provided* pursuant to a plan of care *prescribed* by a licensed health care practitioner.

A chronically ill individual is defined as someone who has been certified within the previous 12 months by a **licensed health care practitioner** and who:

- Is unable to perform (without substantial assistance) at least two activities of daily living (ADL – eating, toileting, transferring, bathing, dressing, and continence) for at least 90 days due to a loss of functional capacity.
- Has a similar level of disability as determined under regulations prescribed by the secretary of the Treasury in consultation with the

Secretary of Health and Human Services.

- Requires substantial supervision to protect such individual from threats to health and safety due to severe cognitive impairment.

Let's expand on some of these terms and phrases used above:

A **licensed health care practitioner** is a physician, registered nurse, licensed social worker, or another individual who meets such requirements as may be prescribed by the Secretary of the Treasury.

HIPPA (Health Insurance Portability and Accountability Act) cleared up many of the uncertainties as to whether various expenditures for home care qualified for the medical expense deduction.

Now, qualified long-term care services include maintenance or personal care services. This is the type of care provided in Adult Family Homes. At least in Washington State, Adult Family Homes are required to have a written care plan, a necessary provision for tax deductibility.

Maintenance and personal care services are defined as care for which its primary purpose is providing a chronically ill individual with needed assistance with his or her disabilities (including protection from threats to health and safety due to severe cognitive impairment).

These services include meal preparation, household cleaning, and similar services that a chronically ill person is unable to perform. The services do not have to be performed in a nursing home, nor must they be performed by a licensed medical professional. As long as the services are provided under a plan of care prescribed by a licensed healthcare practitioner, the cost of an attendant to assist a chronically ill person in his or her daily living activities qualifies.

For Those with Cognitive Impairment and Dementia
For those individuals who are physically able, but have a cognitive impairment such as Alzheimer's disease or other irreversible loss of mental capacity, it is different, but treated similarly to individuals who are unable to perform (without substantial assistance) at least two activities of daily living.

Because eligibility for the medical expense deduction should not be diagnosis-driven, the provision requires that the cognitive impairment must be severe. Severe cognitive impairment means a deterioration or loss in intellectual capacity measured by clinical evidence and tests. These tests should reliably measure impairment in short or long term memory; orientation to people, place and/or time; and deductive or abstract reasoning.

One test commonly used to screen for cognitive impairment is the brief 30-point questionnaire called MMSE (Mini-Mental State Examination). Such a deterioration or loss places the individual in jeopardy of harming himself or others and, therefore, requires substantial supervision by another individual.

In the past, amounts paid to Nursing Homes qualified as medical expenses only if medical care was the principle reason for the stay, or, if not the principle reason, only that part of the cost of care attributable to medical care qualified (not meals and lodging). The enactment of an IRS code included qualified long-term care within the definition of "medical care." This means that amounts paid to long-term care facilities (Adult Family Homes, Nursing Homes, and Assisted Living Facilities) can qualify as medical expenses, provided the person meets either the activities of daily living (ADL) or cognitive impairment requirements and the costs are pursuant to a plan of care prescribed by a health care practitioner.

For residents who are not chronically ill, fees paid to retirement communities and assisted living facilities are deductible as medical expenses to the extent that they are attributable to medical care. The deduction applies to entrance or initiation fees if a portion of the fee is attributable to providing medical services. The facility is responsible for determining the portion of fees allocated to medical care and should provide this information to the residents annually.

If YOU provide financial assistance to an elderly parent, that expense can also be tax-deductible.
The following is an excerpt from the IRS website:

Claiming an Elderly Individual as a Dependent

To claim an individual as a dependent, there are two important qualifications. First, the tax filer (usually a family member) must have provided at least half of the dependent's financial support for the year, and second, the dependent must be related or have lived with the tax filer for one full year.

An important exception exists to the requirement that the tax filer provide at least half of the financial support. If several family members together contribute 50% of the dependent's support, then the family can choose a single member to claim the individual in need of care as a dependent. This is referred to as creating a "Multiple Support Declaration."

Another disclosure: these interpretations are based on talking with our accountant, and reading the law and Congressional Conference Committee reports. I strongly recommend that you check with your own tax advisor.

Learn more about long-term care and tax deductions on the IRS site at Credit for the Elderly or the Disabled (IRS publication 524).

Appendix 4

Getting Your Parents' Financial Affairs in Order

When is it time to deal with that? Now!

How much do you know about your parents' personal and financial arrangements?

Have they been proactive in planning their future? Have you been included in their conversations? And, most importantly, will you be ready to oversee their affairs when they are unable to care for themselves?

In a best case scenario, these conversations would take place while your parent or loved one is fairly young, healthy, and there isn't a lot of reality around becoming "old" —that happens to other people!

The beauty in having these conversations early is that they can be less emotional. You get a clear, unvarnished look at what is most important to your loved one from a realistic point of view, not from a fear or emergency-based position.

It's never too late so if you haven't, let's get you started!

In this section I provide some guidelines to help you through the process.

I'll share the top 3 most important steps you should take with respect to assembling pertinent planning information and document gathering and distribution.

Top 3 Most Important Steps:
1. Establish a joint relationship in your parent or loved one's general checking account.
2. Locate or draft a will (not necessary if there is no estate to distribute, other than personal effects).
3. **Obtain a Health Directive and Durable Power of Attorney (POA or DPOA) – This will allow you to gather information, communicate with agencies, and represent your parent or loved one while working on their behalf, eventually allowing you to make decisions as they become**

incapacitated or unable. As long as the senior is able, they will maintain a role in decision-making. If possible, make these roles effective immediately upon completion of the document.

Information Gathering:

In terms of financial standing and wealth management for each individual, it's important to know what will happen financially to the remaining partner when the other one passes.

Will a pension or disability payment stop or be reduced with the death of a partner? Do they have financial holdings, and if so, how long are they expected to last when using inflationary projections? Are they financially able to remain at home through end of life or will they need to consider a long term care facility? Take a **realistic** look early on.

How much time are you willing to be directly involved daily? What environment would be financially and emotionally suited to their personality and lifestyle, and what are their long-term care options? Are they highly social or do they tend to keep to themselves in a quiet environment?

Documents you should collect or have access to:
1. Original copy of POA and Health Directive – be sure you have at least 3 original copies made when drawn up
2. Original copy of Military Service Discharge
3. Original copy of Benefit Disclosure letters: Social Security, Labor and Industries (L&I) and/or Veterans Insurance or disability, pension(s)
4. Other Income: financial holdings statements
5. Original copy of Will
6. Deeds or contracts for home and properties

Advance Directive and Durable Power of Attorney for Healthcare can be completed by an attorney or on your own (online form and instructions are available). If you live in Washington State, I highly recommend to you complete a POLST Form.

Fill out Five Wishes, the National Advance Directive Day created by the nonprofit organization Aging with Dignity. It's an easy to use legal document that's valuable to have on file. You can also visit the National Library of Medicine.

Distribution of Durable Power of Attorney – Nearly everyone you communicate with on your loved one's behalf will want a copy on file before they'll talk with you. Plan to distribute copies of the DPOA to:

1. Doctors & Hospital
2. Insurance: Health, Car, Home
3. AARP
4. State: DSHS or L&I if they apply
5. Pensions & Holdings
6. Bank
7. Attorney & Money Managers
8. Veterans Administration/U.S. Department of Veterans Affairs (VA)

Please note that the SSA does not accept DPOA – see Representative Payee below.

Social Security – Representative Payee

Power of Attorney does not give legal authority to negotiate and manage a beneficiary's Social Security and/or Supplemental Security Income (SSI) payments. A representative payee is an individual or organization appointed by SSA to receive Social Security and/or SSI benefits for someone who cannot manage or direct someone else to manage his or her money. In order to become a representative payee, a person or organization must apply for and be appointed by the SSA.

Veterans Aid and Assistance – Does your loved one qualify?

For information, see Financial Aid for War Era Veterans and Surviving Spouses.

Wartime veterans and their surviving spouses, 65 years and older, may be entitled to a tax-free benefit called Aid and Attendance. This benefit was designed to provide financial assistance to help offset the cost of long-term care in an assisted living facility or for in home care.

Department of Social and Health Services/Medicaid

Website: Aging & Disability Services Administration/DSHS/Medicaid

Find in-home services, residential care (adult family home, assisted living, nursing home), resources to pay for care, possible state and federal benefits, legal and financial planning, and aging and health information through Aging & Disability Services Administration (ADSA).

You'll also find a Caregivers Resource tab on the DSHS site for the non-paid caregiver (that would be you, most likely). Accessible by phone or in person by appointment, they're generally very helpful and the source of a wealth of information on most topics, including emotional support.

If you expect to, or have already, become involved in the care of your parent(s) or loved one it may be time for you to get the ball rolling. Sooner is definitely better than later.
TAKE ACTION NOW!

Appendix 5

Abbreviations Spelled Out

Here is a quick guide to the many abbreviations and acronyms used in this book:

ADLs	Activities of Daily Living
ADSA	Aging & Disability Services Administration
AFH	Adult Family Home
AL	Assisted Living
ALC	Assisted Living Care
ALF	Assisted Living Facility
ARC	Adult Residential Care
ARNP	Advanced Registered Nurse Practitioner
BSN	Bachelor's in Nursing
CNA or NAC	Certified Nursing Assistant (former title); current title is NA-C
CPR	Cardio Pulmonary Resuscitation
CSA	Certified Senior Advisor
DNP	Doctor of Nursing Practice
DPOA	Durable Power of Attorney
POA	Power of Attorney
DOH	Department of Health
DSHS	Department of Social Health Services
EARC	Enhanced Adult Residential Care
ECS	Expanded Community Services
FTC	Federal Trade Commission
HIPPA	Health Insurance Portability and Accountability Act
IRS	Internal Revenue Service
L&I	Labor and Industries
LPN	Licensed Practical Nurse
LTC	Long Term Care
MMSE	Mini Mental State Examination
MSW	Master of Social Work
NAR	Nursing Assistant – Registered

NAC   Nursing Assistant – Certified; formerly CNA – Certified Nursing Assistant

POA   Power of Attorney, also: DPOA – Durable Power of Attorney

NCLEX – PN   National Council Licensure Examination – Practical

NCLEX - RN   Nurse / Registered Nurse

RCW   Revised Code of Washington

RN   Registered Nurse

SSA   Social Security Administration

SSI   Supplemental Security Income

VA   Veterans Administration/U.S. Department of Veterans Affairs

WAC   Washington Administrative Code

WSRCC   Washington State Residential Care Council

My Story

I was born in Sicily and my parents immigrated to Geneva, Switzerland, when I was about four years old to escape severe poverty and unemployment. But, Sicily always remained home. So, twice a year during Christmas and in summer time we made the journey back south some 1250 miles, by car and boat. That's when I learned to drive, at about twelve years old.

Despite very modest means we never lacked food or a roof over our heads. I feel blessed to have been raised in a family-centered culture, surrounded by a large number of aunts, uncles, and cousins. Twenty-two first-degree aunts and uncles, to be exact. To this day, several of them still treat me as their own son, even scolding me if I don't visit or at least call! There were always family around to share the role of taking care of the home and watching the children. Very early, I learned that grandparents and surrogate caregivers were an important part of a healthy functioning and loving family dynamic.

Just before I turned 18, my father put in a word for me at University Hospital in Geneva where he worked. And voilà – 2 months after my 18th birthday, I was gainfully employed working with the elderly. I hadn't chosen that particular field of work or job, but I quickly discovered how much I enjoyed it. I was good at relating to and communicating with seniors. I made them laugh – something that made us both feel good. I eventually moved to the emergency room department, with rotations in orthopedics and rehabilitation.

At twenty-two, I took my first trip to America (California). I didn't know a single word of English, and just before returning home to Switzerland I met an amazing woman who spoke perfect French—lucky me! I invited her to join me in Switzerland and just one year later, she came. We were married there, six months after her arrival.

At my urging we moved back to the United States and arrived in Seattle in 1989. We were completely broke and knew one person. My English wasn't perfect, but I was learning. I found a job at a local nursing home and earned $6.12 per hour. Even then, that was not enough to lift us out of poverty.

"When a coworker-friend mentioned the "adult family home" model, my creative mind was instantly engaged as I considered taking the needs of so many seniors and their loved ones, blending them with my skills and quality standards I was accustomed to from Switzerland. Not only could I make a tangible contribution to my community, but there was (and still is) a very real need for a long-term care that centers around the individual who needs care, rather than forcing the individual to adapt to the care setting's institutional structure. And, it was the perfect solution to my family getting into thriving mode, rather than simply surviving!

I clearly remember my very first resident, Vander; he loved holding our youngest, Natalie, on his lap and singing her lullabies when she was just a few weeks old. Even though he had a terrible singing voice, the love and joy on his face was undeniable, and our baby Natalie soaked in every bit of it! He later told me that his only daughter, Rose, had Down syndrome and he wasn't able to experience that bond during her infancy, and he now felt he'd come full circle and found completion. He passed shortly thereafter.

Now twenty-three years later, I'm still so grateful for the opportunity to serve the elderly population and to help relieve the burden of care from their adult children. I truly believe that helping another human being is one of the most important and noble jobs anyone can have.

Smaller is Better
Here is what drew me so powerfully to the Adult Family Home model. During my work at the nursing home, I normally cared for 8 to 12 residents, and double that when short-staffed. By focusing my full-time effort to care for only 6 clients in an AFH model, I knew I could bring them the kind of top-notch care and attention I was accustomed to providing in Switzerland. Being in a real home rather than an institution fosters an atmosphere of family and kinship that most of us were brought up in. It's familiar, familial, and therefore instinctively appealing. Having several generations co-exist under one roof is natural in many cultures and adds richness to life.

If you are anything like me, you want your parent to live in a home that cares for him or her like family. You want them to be cared for by people who embrace who they are with care and compassion. A place that understands what it's like to be in your shoes as the adult child.

And that is exactly how I run Spada Homes, and the approach I take when consulting other care providers.

As an attorney friend of mine says, "It's not enough to care for a resident, you must care about the resident."

There is a lot of wisdom in those words and I hope this brief writing will support you in finding just that, a home for your loved one who will not only care *for* her, but *about* her.

9 7 9 8 7 2 8 7 8 5 5 2 1